A CALL TO THE UNCONVERTED

RICHARD BAXTER

BAKER BOOK HOUSE
Grand Rapids, Michigan

Paperback edition issued 1976
by Baker Book House

ISBN: 0-8010-0674-0

PHOTOLITHOPRINTED BY CUSHING - MALLOY, INC.
ANN ARBOR, MICHIGAN, UNITED STATES OF AMERICA
1976

CONTENTS

THE GREAT SUCCESS WHICH ATTENDED THE
CALL WHEN FIRST PUBLISHED.

It may be proper to prefix an account of this book given by Mr. Baxter himself, which was found in his study, after his death, in his own words:

"I published a short treatise on conversion, entitled, A Call to the Unconverted. The occasion of this was my converse with Bishop Usher while I was at London; who, approving my method and directions for Peace of Conscience, was importunate with me to write directions suited to the various states of Christians, and also against particular sins. I reverenced the man, but disregarded these persuasions, supposing I could do nothing but what is done better already: but when he was dead, his words went deeper to my mind, and I purposed to obey his counsel; yet, so as that to the first sort of men, the ungodly, I thought vehement persuasions meeter than directions only; and so for such I published this little book, which God hath blessed with unexpected success, beyond all the rest that I have written, except The Saint's Rest. In a little more than a year there were about twenty thousand of them printed by my own consent, and about ten thousand since, beside many thousands by stolen impressions, which poor men stole for lucre's sake. Through God's mercy I have information of almost whole households converted by this small book which I set so light by; and, as if all this in England, Scotland, and Ireland, were not mercy enough to me, God, since I was silenced, hath sent it over in his message to many beyond the seas; for when

Mr. Elliot had printed all the Bible in the Indian language, he next translated this my *Call to the Unconverted*, as he wrote to us here. And yet God would make some farther use of it; for Mr. Stoop, the pastor of the French Church in London, being driven hence by the displeasure of his superiors, was pleased to translate it into French. I hope it will not be unprofitable there; nor in Germany, where also it has been printed."

It may be proper further to mention Dr. Bates' account of the author, and of this useful treatise. In his sermon at Mr. BAXTER's funeral, he thus says: "His books of practical divinity have been effectual for more conversions of sinners to God than any printed in our time: and while the church remains on earth, will be of continual efficacy to recover lost souls. There is a vigorous pulse in them, that keeps the reader awake and attentive. His Call to the Unconverted, how small in bulk, but how powerful in virtue! Truth speaks in it with that authority and efficacy, that it makes the reader to lay his hand upon his heart, and find that he has a soul and a conscience, though he lived before as if he had none. He told some friends, that six brothers were converted by reading that CALL; and that every week he received letters of some converted by his books. This he spake with most humble thankfulness, that God was pleased to use him as an instrument for the salvation of souls."

A CALL
TO THE UNCONVERTED.

EZEKIEL, XXXIII. 11.

*Say unto them, As I live, saith the Lord God, I have
no pleasure in the death of the wicked; but that
the wicked turn from his way and live: turn ye
turn ye from your evil ways; for why will ye die,
O house of Israel?*

It hath been the astonishing wonder of many a
man as well as me, to read in the Holy Scriptures how
few will be saved, and that the greatest part even of
those that are called, will be everlastingly shut out of
the kingdom of heaven, and be tormented with the
devils in eternal fire. Infidels believe not this when
they read it, and therefore they must feel it; those
that do believe it are forced to cry out with Paul,
(Rom. 11. 13,) "O the depth of the riches both of the
wisdom and knowledge of God! How unsearchable
are his judgments, and his ways past finding out!"
But nature itself doth teach us all to lay the blame
of evil works upon the doers; and therefore when we
see any heinous thing done, a principle of justice doth
provoke us to inquire after him that did it, that the
evil of the work may return the evil of shame upon
the author. If we saw a man killed and cut in pieces
by the way, we would presently ask, Oh! who did
this cruel deed? If the town was wilfully set on fire,
you would ask, what wicked wretch did this? So
when we read that many souls will be miserable in
hell for ever, we must needs think with ourselves, how
comes this to pass? and whose fault is it? Who is it

that is so cruel as to be the cause of such a thing as this? and we can meet with few that will own the guilt. It is indeed confessed by all, that Satan is the cause; but that doth not resolve the doubt, because he is not the principal cause. He doth not force men to sin, but tempts them to it, and leaves it to their own wills whether they will do it or not. He doth not carry men to an alehouse and force open their mouths and pour in the drink; nor doth he hold them that they cannot go to God's service; nor doth he force their hearts from holy thoughts. It lieth therefore between God himself and the sinner; one of them must needs be the principal cause of all this misery, whichever it is, for there is no other to lay it upon; and God disclaimeth it; he will not take it upon him; and the wicked disclaim it usually, and they will not take it upon them, and this is the controversy that is here managing in my text.

The Lord complaineth of the people; and the people think it is the fault of God. The same controversy is handled, chap. 18. 25: they plainly say, "that the way of the Lord is not equal." So here they say, verse 19, "If our transgressions and our sins be upon us, and we pine away in them, how shall we then live?' As if they should say, if we must die, and be miserable, how can we help it? as if it were not their fault, but God's. But God, in my text, doth clear himself of it, and telleth them how they may help it if they will, and persuadeth them to use the means, and if they will not be persuaded, he lets them know that it is the fault of themselves; and if this will not satisfy them, he will not forbear to punish them. It is he that will be the Judge, and he will judge them according to their ways; they are no judge of him or of themselves, as wanting authority, and wisdom, and impartiality; nor is it the cavilling and quarrelling with God that shall serve their turn, or save them from the execution of justice, at which they murmur.

The words of this verse contain, 1. God's purgation or clearing himself from the blame of their destruction. This he doth not by disowning his law, that the wicked shall die, nor by disowning his judgments and execution according to that law, or giving them any hope that the law shall not be executed; but by professing that it is not their death that he takes pleasure in, but their returning rather, that they may live; and this he confirmeth to them by his oath. 2. An express exhortation to the wicked to return; wherein God doth not only command, but persuade and condescend also to reason the case with them. Why will they die? The direct end of this exhortation is, that they may turn and live. The secondary or reserved ends, upon supposition that this is not attained, are these two: First, To convince them by the means which he used, that it is not the fault of God if they be miserable. Secondly, To convince them from their manifest wilfulness in rejecting all his commands and persuasions, that it is the fault of themselves, and they die, even because they will die.

The substance of the text doth lie in these observations following:—

Doctrine 1. It is the unchangeable law of God, that wicked men must turn or die.

Doctrine 2. It is the promise of God, that the wicked shall live, if they will but turn.

Doctrine 3. God takes pleasure in men's conversion and salvation, but not in their death or damnation: he had rather they would return and live, than go on and die.

Doctrine 4. This is a most certain truth, which because God would not have men to question, he hath confirmed it to them solemnly by his oath.

Doctrine 5. The Lord doth redouble his commands and persuasions to the wicked to turn.

Doctrine 6. The Lord condescendeth to reason the case with them; and asketh the wicked why they will die?

Doctrine 7. If after all this the wicked will not turn, it is not the fault of God that they perish, but of themselves; their own wilfulness is the cause of their own damnation; they therefore die because they will die.

Having laid the text open in these propositions, I shall next speak somewhat of each of them in order. though briefly.

DOCTRINE I

It is the unchangeable law of God, that wicked men must turn, or die.

If you will believe God, believe this: there is but one of these two ways for every wicked man, either conversion or damnation. I know the wicked will hardly be persuaded either of the truth or equity of this. No wonder if the guilty quarrel with the law. Few men are apt to believe that which they would not have to be true, and fewer would have that to be true which they apprehended to be against them. But it is not quarrelling with the law, or with the judge, that will save the malefactor. Believing and regarding the law, might have prevented his death; but denying and accusing it will but hasten it. If it were not so, a hundred would bring their reason against the law, for one that would bring his reason to the law, and men would rather choose to give their reasons why they should not be punished, than to hear the commands and reasons of their governors which require them to obey. The law was not made for you to judge, but that you might be ruled and judged by it.

But if there be any so blind as to venture to question either the truth or the justice of this law of God, I shall briefly give you that evidence of both which methinks, should satisfy a reasonable man.

And first, if you doubt whether this be the word of God, or not, besides a hundred other texts, you may be satisfied by these few:—Matt. 18: 3. "Verily I say unto you, except ye be converted and become as little children, ye cannot enter into the kingdom of God." John 3: 3. "Verily, verily, I say unto you, except a man be born again he cannot see the kingdom of God." 2 Cor. 5: 17. "If any man be in Christ, he is a new creature; old things are passed away; behold, all things are become new." Col. 3: 9, 10. "Ye have put off the old man with his deeds, and have put on the new man, which is renewed in knowledge after the image of him that created him." Heb. 12: 14. "Without holiness no man shall see the Lord." Rom. 8: 8, 9. "So then they that are in the flesh cannot please God. Now if any man have not the spirit of Christ, he is none of his." Gal. 6: 15. "For in Christ Jesus neither circumcision availeth any thing, nor uncircumcision, but a new creature." 1 Pet. 1: 3. "According to his abundant grace he hath begotten us to a lively hope." Ver. 23. "Being born again, not of corruptible seed, but of incorruptible, by the word of God, which liveth and abideth for ever."

1 Pet. 2: 1, 2. "Wherefore laying aside all malice, and all guile, and hypocrisies, and envies, and evil speaking, as new born babes, desire the sincere milk of the word, that ye may grow thereby." Psalm 9: 17. " The wicked shall be turned into hell, and all the nations that forget God." Psalm 11: 4. "And the Lord loveth the righteous, but the wicked his soul hateth."

As I need not stay to open these texts which are so plain, so I think I need not add any more of that multitude which speak the like. If, thou be a man that dost believe the word of God, here is already enough to satisfy thee that the wicked must be converted or condemned. You are already brought so far, that you must either confess that this is true, or say plainly, you will not believe the word of God. And if once you be come to that pass, there is but small hopes of you: look to yourself as well as you can, for it is like you will not be long out of hell. You would be ready to fly in the face of him that should give you the lie; and yet dare you give the lie to God? But if you tell God plainly you will not believe him, blame him not if he never warn you more, or if he forsake you, and give you up as hopeless; for to what purpose should he warn you, if you will not believe him? Should he send an angel from heaven to you, it seems you would not believe. For an angel can speak but the word of God; and if an angel should bring you any other gospel, you are not to receive it, but to hold him accursed. Gal. 1: 8. And surely there is no angel to be believed before the Son of God, who came from the Father to bring us this doctrine. If He be not to be believed, then all the angels in heaven are not to be believed. And if you stand on these terms with God, I shall leave you till he deal with you in a more convincing way. God hath a voice that will make you hear. Though he entreat you to hear the voice of his gospel, he will make you hear the voice of his condemning sentence, without entreaty. We cannot make you believe against your wills; but God will make you feel against your wills.

But let us hear what reason you have why you will not believe this word of God, which tells us that the wicked must be converted, or condemned. I know your reason; it is because that you judge it unlikely that God should be so unmerciful: you think it cruelty to damn men everlastingly for so small a thing as a sinful life. And this leads us to the second thing, which is to justify the equity of God in his laws and judgments.

And first, I think you will not deny that it is most suitable to an immortal soul to be ruled by laws that promise an immortal reward, and threaten an endless punishment. Otherwise the law should not be suited to the nature of the subject, who will not be fully ruled by any lower means than the hopes or fears of everlasting things: as it is in cases of temporal punishment, if a law were now made that the most heinous crimes shall be punished with a hundred years' captivity, this might be of some efficacy, as being equal to our lives. But, if there had been no other penalties before the flood, when men lived eight or nine hundred years, it would not have been sufficient, because men would know that they might have so many hundred years impunity afterward. So it is in our present case.

2. I suppose that you will confess, that the promise of an endless and inconceivable glory is not so unsuit-

able to the wisdom of God, or the case of man: and why then should you not think so of the threatening of an endless and unspeakable misery !

3. When you find it in the word of God that so it is, and so it will be, do ye think yourselves fit to contradict this word? Will you call your Maker to the bar, and examine his word upon the accusation of falsehood? Will you sit upon him and judge him by the law of your conceits? Are you wiser, and better, and more righteous than he? Must the God of heaven come to school to you to learn wisdom? Must Infinite Wisdom learn of folly, and Infinite Goodness be corrected by a sinner that cannot keep himself an hour clean? Must the Almighty stand at the bar of a worm? O horrid arrogancy of senseless dust! shall ever mole, or clod, or dunghill, accuse the sun of darkness, and undertake to illuminate the world? Where were you when the Almighty made the laws, that he did not call you to his counsel? Surely he made them before you were born, without desiring your advice; and you came into the world too late to reverse them, if you could have done so great a work. You should have stepped out of your nothingness and have contradicted Christ when he was on earth, or Moses before him, or have saved Adam and his sinful progeny from the threatened death, that so there might have been no need of Christ. And what if God withdraw his patience and sustaining power, and let you drop into hell while you are quarrelling with his word, will you then believe that there is a hell?

4. If sin be such an evil that it requireth the death of Christ for its expiation, no wonder if it deserve our everlasting misery.

5. And if the sin of the devils deserved an endless torment, why not also the sin of man?

6. And methinks you should perceive that it is not possible for the best of men, much less for the wicked, to be competent judges of the desert of sin. Alas! we are both blind and partial. You can never know fully the desert of sin, till you fully know the evil of sin; and you can never fully know the evil of sin, till you fully know, 1. The excellency of the soul which it deformeth. 2. And the excellency of holiness which it obliterates. 3. The reason and excellency of the law which it violates. 4. The excellency of the glory which it despises. 5. The excellency and office of reason which it treadeth down. 6. No, nor till you know the infinite excellency, almightiness and holiness of that God against whom it is committed. When you fully know all these, you shall fully know the desert of sin besides. You know that the offender is too partial to judge the law, or the proceeding of his judge. We judge by feeling which blinds our reason. We see, in common worldly things, that most men think the cause is right which is their own, and that all is wrong that is done against them; and let the most wise or just impartial friends persuade them to the contrary, and it is all in vain. There are few children but think the father is unmerciful, or dealeth hardly with them if he whip them. There is scarce the vilest wretch but thinketh the church doth wrong him if they excommunicate him: or scarce a thief or murderer that is hanged, but would accuse the law and judge of cruelty, if that would serve their turn.

7. Can you think that an unholy soul is fit for heaven? Alas, they cannot love God here, nor do him any service which he can accept. They are contrary

to God, they loathe that which he most loveth, and love that which he abhorreth. They are incapable of that imperfect communion with Him which his saints here partake of. How then can they live in that perfect love of him, and full delight and communion with him, which is the blessedness of heaven? You do not accuse yourselves of unmercifulness, if you make not your enemy your bosom counsellor; or if you take not your swine to bed and board with you: no, nor if you take away his life though he never sinned; and yet you will blame the absolute Lord, the most wise and gracious Sovereign of the world, if he condemn the unconverted to perpetual misery.

Use.—I beseech you now, all that love your souls, that, instead of quarrelling with God and with his word, you will presently receive it, and use it for your good. All you that are yet unconverted, take this as the undoubted truth of God:—You must, ere long, be converted or condemned; there is no other way but to turn, or die. When God, that cannot lie, hath told you this; when you hear it from the Maker and Judge of the world, it is time for him that hath ears, to hear. By this time you may see what you have to trust to. You are but dead and damned men, except you will be converted. Should I tell you otherwise, I should deceive you with a lie. Should I hide this from you, I should undo you, and be guilty of your blood, as the verses before my text assure me.—Verse 8. "When I say to the wicked man, O wicked man, thou shalt surely die; if thou dost not speak to warn the wicked from his way, that wicked man shall die in his iniquity; but his blood will I require at thine hand." You see then, though this be a rough and unwelcome doctrine, it is such as we must preach, and you must hear. It is easier to hear of hell than feel it. If your necessities did not require it, we would not gall your tender ears with truths that seem so harsh and grievous. Hell would not be so full, if people were but willing to know their case, and to hear and think of it. The reason why so few escape it, is because they strive not to enter in at the strait gate of conversion, and go the narrow way of holiness, while they have time: and they strive not, because they are not awakened to a lively feeling of the danger they are in; and they are not awakened because they are loth to hear or think of it: and that is partly through foolish tenderness and carnal self-love, and partly because they do not well believe the word that threateneth it. If you will not thoroughly believe this truth, methinks the weight of it should force you to remember it, and it should follow you, and give you no rest till you are converted. If you had but once heard this word by the voice of an angel, " Thou must be converted, or condemned : turn, or die :" would it not stick in your mind, and haunt you night and day ? so that in your sinning you would remember it, as if the voice were still in your ears, " Turn, or die !" O happy were your soul if it might thus work with you and never be forgotten, or let you alone till it have driven home your heart to God. But if you will cast it out by forgetfulness or unbelief, how can it work to your conversion and salvation? But take this with you to your sorrow, though you may put this out of your mind, you cannot put it out of the Bible, but there it will stand as a sealed truth, which you shall experimentally know for ever, that there is no other way but, "turn, or die."

O what is the matter then that the hearts of sin-

ners are not pierced with such a weighty truth? A
man would think now, that every unconverted soul
that hears these words should be pricked to the heart,
and think with himself, 'This is my own case,' and
never be quiet till he found himself converted. Believe
it, this drowsy careless temper will not last long. Conversion and condemnation are both of them awaken-
ing things, and one of them will make you feel ere
long. I can foretell it as truly as if I saw it with my
eyes, that either grace or hell will shortly bring these
matters to the quick, and make you say, "What have
I done? what a foolish wicked course have I taken?"
The scornful and the stupid state of sinners will last
but a little while: as soon as they either turn or die,
the presumptuous dream will be at an end, and then
their wits and feeling will return.

But I foresee there are two things that are likely to
harden the unconverted, and make me lose all my
labor, except they can be taken out of the way; and
that is the misunderstanding on those two words, the
wicked and *turn*. Some will think to themselves,
'It is true, the wicked must turn or die; but what is
that to me, I am not wicked; though I am a sinner,
all men are.' Others will think, 'It is true that we
must turn from our evil ways, but I am turned long
ago; I hope this is not now to do.' And thus while
wicked men think they are not wicked, but are already converted, we lose all our labor in persuading
them to turn. I shall therefore, before I go any further, tell you here who are meant by the wicked;
and who they are that must turn or die; and also
what is meant by turning, and who they are that are
truly converted. And this I have purposely reserved
for this place, preferring the method that fits my end

And here you may observe, that in the sense of the text, a wicked man and a converted man are contraries. No man is a wicked man that is converted; and no man is a converted man that is wicked; so that to be a wicked man and to be an unconverted man, is all one; and therefore in opening one, we shall open both.

Before I can tell you what either wickedness or conversion is, I must go to the bottom, and fetch up the matter from the beginning.

It pleased the great Creator of the world to make three sorts of living creatures. Angels he made pure spirits without flesh, and therefore he made them only for heaven, and not to dwell on earth. Brutes were made flesh, without immortal souls, and therefore they were made only for earth, and not for heaven. Man is of a middle nature, between both, as partaking of both flesh and spirit, and therefore he was made both for heaven and earth. But as his flesh is made to be but a servant to his spirit, so is he made for earth but as his passage or way to heaven, and not that this should be his home or happiness. The blessed state that man was made for, was to behold the glorious majesty of the Lord, and to praise him among his Holy Angels, and to love him, and to be filled with his love for ever. And as this was the end that man was made for, so God did give him means that were fitted to the attaining of it. These means were principally two: First, the right inclination and disposition of the mind of man. Secondly, The right ordering of his life and practice. For the first, God suited the disposition of man unto his end, giving him such knowledge of God as was fit for his present state, and a heart disposed and inclined to God in holy love. But yet he did not fix or confirm him in this condition, but, having made him a free agent, he left him in the hands of his own free will. For the second, God did that which belonged to him; that is, he gave him a perfect law, required him to continue in the love of God, and perfectly to obey him. By the wilful breach of this law, man did not only forfeit his hopes of everlasting life, but also turned his heart from God, and fixed it on these lower fleshly things, and hereby blotted out the spiritual image of God from his soul; so that man did both fall short of the glory of God, which was his end, and put himself out of the way by which he should have attained it, and this both as to the frame of his heart, and of his life. The holy inclination and love of his soul to God, he lost, and instead of it he contracted an inclination and love to the pleasing of his flesh, or carnal self, by earthly things; growing strange to God and acquainted with the creature. And the course of this life was suited to the bent and inclination of his heart; he lived to his carnal self, and not to God; he sought the creature, for the pleasing of his flesh, instead of seeking to please the Lord. With this nature or corrupt inclination, we are all now born into the world; " for who can bring a clean thing out of an unclean?" Job, 14 : 4. As a lion hath a fierce and cruel nature before he doth devour; and an adder hath a venomous nature before she sting, so in our infancy we have those sinful natures or inclinations, before we think, or speak, or do amiss. And hence springeth all the sin of our lives; and not only so, but when God hath, of his mercy, provided us a remedy, even the Lord Jesus Christ, to be the Savior of our souls, and bring us back to God again, we naturally love our present state, and are loth to be brought out of it, and therefore are set against the means of our recovery: and though custom hath taught us to thank Christ for his good-will, yet carnal self persuades us to refuse his remedies, and to desire to be excused when we are commanded to take the medicines which he offers, and are called to forsake all and follow him to God and glory.

I pray you read over this leaf again, and mark it; for in these few words you have a true description of our natural state, and consequently of wicked man; for every man that is in the state of corrupted nature is a wicked man, and in a state of death.

By this also you are prepared to understand what it is to be converted: to which end you must further know, that the mercy of God, not willing that man should perish in his sin, provided a remedy, by causing his Son to take our nature, and being, in one person, God and man, to become a mediator between God and man; and by dying for our sins on the cross, to ransom us from the curse of God and the power of the devil. And having thus redeemed us, the Father hath delivered us into his hands as his own. Hereupon the Father and the Mediator do make a new law and covenant for man, not like the first, which gave life to none but the perfectly obedient, and condemned man for every sin; but Christ hath made a law of grace, or a promise of pardon and everlasting life to all that, by true repentance, and by faith in Christ, are converted unto God; like an act of oblivion, which is made by a prince to a company of rebels, on condition they will lay down their arms and come in and be loyal subjects for the time to come.

But, because the Lord knoweth that the heart of man is grown so wicked, that, for all this, men will not accept of the remedy if they be left to themselves, therefore the Holy Ghost hath undertaken it as his office to inspire the Apostles, and seal the Scriptures by miracles and wonders, and to illuminate and convert the souls of the elect.

So by this much you see, that as there are three persons in the Trinity, the Father, the Son, and the Holy Ghost, so each of these persons have their several works, which are eminently ascribed to them.

The Father's works were, to create us, to rule us, as his rational creatures, by the law of nature, and judge us thereby; and in mercy to provide us a Redeemer when we were lost; and to send his Son, and accept his ransom.

The works of the Son for us were these: to ransom and redeem us by his suffering and righteousness; to give out the promise or law of grace, and rule and judge the world as their Redeemer, on terms of grace: and to make intercession for us, that the benefits of his death may be communicated; and to send the Holy Ghost, which the Father also doth by the Son.

The works of the Holy Ghost, for us, are these: to indite the Holy Scriptures, by inspiring and guiding the Apostles, and sealing the word, by his miraculous gifts and works, and the illuminating and exciting the ordinary ministers of the gospel, and so enabling them and helping them to publish that word; and by the same word illuminating and converting the souls of men. So that as you could not have been reasonable creatures, if the Father had not created you, nor have had any access to God, if the Son had not died, so neither can you have a part in Christ, or be saved, except the Holy Ghost do sanctify you.

So that by this time you may see the several causes

of this work. The Father sendeth the Son: the Son redeemeth us and maketh the promise of grace: the Holy Ghost inditeth and sealeth this Gospel: the Apostles are the secretaries of the Spirit to write it: the preachers of the Gospel to proclaim it, and persuade men to open it: and the Holy Ghost doth make their preaching effectual, by opening the hearts of men to entertain it. And all this to repair the image of God upon the soul, and to set the heart upon God again, and take it off the creature and carnal self to which it is revolted, and so to turn the current of the life into a heavenly course, which before was earthly; and through this, embracing Christ by faith, who is the Physician of the soul.

By what I have said, you may see what it is to be wicked, and what it is to be converted; which, I think, will yet be plainer to you, if I describe them as consisting of their several parts. And for the first, a wicked man may be known by these three things:

First, He is one who placeth his chief affections on earth, and loveth the creature more than God, and his fleshly prosperity above the heavenly felicity. He savoreth the things of the flesh, but neither discerneth nor savoreth the things of the Spirit; though he will say, that heaven is better than earth, yet he doth not really so esteem it to himself. If he might be sure of earth, he would let go heaven, and had rather stay here than be removed thither. A life of perfect holiness in the sight of God, and in his love and praises for ever in heaven, doth not find such liking with his heart as a life of health, and wealth, and honor here upon earth. And though he falsely profess that he loves God above all, yet indeed he never felt the power of divine love within him, but his mind is more set on worldly or fleshly pleasures than on God. In a word, whoever loves earth above heaven, and fleshly prosperity more than God, is a wicked unconverted man.

On the other hand, a converted man is illuminated to discern the loveliness of God, and so far believeth the glory that is to be had with God, that his heart is taken up with it and set more upon it than any thing in this world. He had rather see the face of God, and live in his everlasting love and praises, than have all the wealth or pleasures of the world. He seeth that all things else are vanity, and nothing but God can fill the soul; and therefore let the world go which way it will, he layeth up his treasures and hopes in heaven, and for that he is resolved to let go all. As the fire doth mount upward, and the needle that is touched with the loadstone still turns to the north, so the converted soul is inclined unto God. Nothing else can satisfy him: nor can he find any content and rest but in his love. In a word, all that are converted do esteem and love God better than all the world, and the heavenly felicity is dearer to them than their fleshly prosperity. The proof of what I have said you may find in these places of Scriptures: Phil. 3 : 18, 21. Matt. 6 : 19, 20, 21. Col. 3 : 1, 4. Rom. 8 : 5, 9, 18, 23. Psalm 73 : 25, 26.

Secondly, A wicked man is one that makes it the principal business of his life to prosper in the world, and attain his fleshly ends. And though he may read, and hear, and do much in the outward duties of religion, and forbear disgraceful sins, yet this is all but by-the-by, and he never makes it the principal business of his life to please God, and attain everlasting glory, and puts off God with the leavings of the world, and gives him no more service than the flesh can spare, for he will not part with all for heaven.

On the contrary, a converted man is one that makes it the principal care and business of his life to please God, and to be saved, and takes all the blessings of this life but as accommodations in his journey toward another life, and useth the creature in subordination to God; he loves a holy life, and longs to be more holy; he hath no sin but what he hateth, and longeth, and prayeth, and striveth to be rid of. The drift and bent of his life is for God, and if he sin, it is contrary to the very bent of his heart and life; and therefore he riseth again and lamenteth it, and dares not wilfully live in any known sin. There is nothing in this world so dear to him but he can give it up to God, and forsake it for him and the hopes of glory. All this you may see in Col. 3 : 1, 5. Matt. 6 : 20, 33. Luke, 18 : 22, 23, 29. Luke, 14 : 18, 24, 26, 27. Rom. 8 : 13. Gal. 5 : 24. Luke 12 : 21, &c.

Thirdly, The soul of a wicked man did never truly discern and relish the mystery of redemption, nor thankfully entertain an offered Savior, nor is he taken up with the love of the Redeemer, nor willing to be ruled by him as the Physician of his soul, that he may be saved from the guilt and power of his sins, and recovered to God; but his heart is insensible of this unspeakable benefit, and is quite against the healing means by which he should be recovered. Though he may be willing to be outwardly religious, yet he never resigns up his soul to Christ, and to the motions and conduct of his word and Spirit.

On the contrary, the converted soul having felt himself undone by sin, and perceiving that he hath lost his peace with God and hopes of heaven, and is in danger of everlasting misery, doth thankfully entertain the tidings of redemption, and believing in the Lord Jesus as his only Savior, resigns himself up to him for wisdom, righteousness, sanctification, and redemption. He takes Christ as the life of his soul, and lives by him, and uses him as a salve for every sore, admiring the wisdom and love of God in this wonderful work of man's redemption. In a word, Christ doth even dwell in his heart by faith, and the life that he now liveth, is by the faith of the Son of God, that loved him, and gave himself for him; yea, it is not so much he that liveth, as Christ in him. For these. see Job, 1 : 11, 12; and 3 : 19, 20. Rom. 8 : 9. Phil. 3 : 7, 10. Gal. 2 : 20. Job, 15 : 2, 3, 4. 1 Cor. 1 : 20. 2 : 2.

You see now, in plain terms from the Word of God, who are the wicked and who are the converted. Ignorant people think, that if a man be no swearer, nor curser, nor railer, nor drunkard, nor fornicator, nor extortioner, nor wrong any body in his dealings, and if he come to church and say his prayers, he cannot be a wicked man. Or if a man that hath been guilty of drunkenness, swearing, or gaming, or the like vices, do but forbear them for the time to come, they think that this is a converted man. Others think if a man that hath been an enemy, and scorner at godliness, do but approve it, and be hated for it by the wicked, as the godly are, that this must needs be a converted man. And some are so foolish as to think that they are converted by taking up some new opinion, and falling into some dividing party. And some think, if they have but been affrighted by the fears of hell, and had convictions of conscience, and thereupon have purposed and promised amendment, and take up a life of civil behavior and outward religion, that this

must needs be true conversion. And these are the
poor deluded souls that are like to lose the benefit of
all our persuasions; and when they hear that the
wicked must turn or die, they think that this is not
spoken to them, for they are not wicked, but are turned
already. And therefore it is that Christ told some of
the rulers of the Jews who were greater and more
civil than the common people, that " publicans and
harlots go into the kingdom of Christ before them."
Matt. 21 : 31. Not that a harlot or gross sinner can
be saved without conversion; but because it was easier
to make these gross sinners perceive their sin and misery, and the necessity of a change, than the more
civil sort, who delude themselves by thinking that
they are converted already, when they are not.

O sirs, conversion is another kind of work than most
are aware of. It is not a small matter to bring an
earthly mind to heaven, and to show man the amiable
excellence of God, till he be taken up in such love to
him that can never be quenched; to break the heart
for sin, and make him fly for refuge to Christ, and
thankfully embrace him as the life of his soul; to have
the very drift and bent of the heart and life changed;
so that a man renounceth that which he took for his
felicity, and placeth his felicity where he never did
before, and lives not to the same end, and drives not
on the same design in the world, as he formerly did.
In a word, he that is in Christ is a " new creature :
old things are passed away: behold, all things are
become new." 2 Cor. 5 : 17. He hath a new understanding, a new will and resolution, new sorrows, and
desires, and love, and delight; new thoughts, new
speeches, new company, (if possible,) and a new conversation. Sin, that before was a jesting matter with

him, is now so odious and terrible to him that he flies
from it as from death. The world, that was so lovely
in his eyes, doth now appear but as vanity and vexa-
tion: God, that was before neglected, is now the only
happiness of his soul : before he was forgotten, and
every lust preferred before him, but now he is set next
the heart, and all things must give place to him ; the
heart is taken up in the attendance and observance
of him, is grieved when he hides his face, and never
thinks itself well without him. Christ himself, that
was wont to be slightly thought of, is now his only
hope and refuge, and he lives upon him as on his
daily bread ; he cannot pray without him, nor rejoice
without him, nor think, nor speak, nor live without
him. Heaven itself, that before was looked upon but
as a tolerable reserve, which he hoped might serve
his turn better than hell, when he could not stay any
longer in the world, is now taken for his home, the
place of his only hope and rest, where he shall see,
and love, and praise that God that hath his heart already. Hell, that did seem before but as a bugbear
to frighten men from sin, doth now appear to be a real
misery that is not to be ventured on, nor jested with.
The works of holiness, of which before he was weary,
and thought to be more than needful, are now both his
recreation, and his business, and the trade that he lives
upon. The Bible, which was before to him but almost
as a common book, is now as the law of God ; as a let-
ter written to him, and subscribed with the name of
the Eternal Majesty ; it is the rule of his thoughts,
and words, and deeds ; the commands are binding, the
threats are dreadful, and the promises of it speak life
to his soul. The godly, that seemed to him but like
other men. are now the most excellent and happy on

earth. And the wicked that were his playfellows are now his grief; and he that could laugh at their sins is readier now to weep for their sin and misery, and to say with those of old, (Psalm 16 : 3; 15 : 4. Phil. 3 : 18.) "But to the saints that are in the earth, and to the excellent, in whom is all my delight." "In whose eyes a vile person is contemned; but he honoreth them that fear the Lord: he that sweareth to his own hurt, and changeth not." "For many walk, of whom I have told you often, and now tell you, even weeping, that they are the enemies of the cross of Christ." In short, he hath a new end in his thoughts, and a new way in his endeavors, and therefore his heart and life are new. Before, his carnal self was his end, and his pleasure and worldly profits and credit were his way; and now God and everlasting glory are his end, and Christ, and the Spirit, and word, and ordinances. Holiness to God, and righteousness and mercy to men, these are his way. Before, self was the chief ruler, to which the matters of God and conscience must stoop and give place; and now God, in Christ, by the Spirit, word and ministry, is the chief ruler, to whom both self and all the matters of self must give place. So that this is not a change in one, or two, or twenty points, but in the whole soul, and in the very end and bent of the conversation. A man may step out of one path into another, and yet have his face the same way, and be still going toward the same place; but it is another matter to turn quite back, and take his journey quite the contrary way, to a contrary place. So it is here; a man may turn from drunkenness, and forsake other gross disgraceful sins, and set upon some duties of religion, and yet be still going to the same end as before, loving his carnal self above all, and giving it still the government of his soul; but when he is converted, this self is denied, and taken down, and God is set up, and his face is turned the contrary way: and he that before was addicted to himself, and lived to himself, is now, by sanctification, devoted to God, and liveth unto God. Before, he asked himself what he should do with his time, his parts, and his estate, and for himself he used them; but now he asketh God what he shall do with them, and useth them for him. Before, he would please God so far as might accord with the pleasure of his flesh and carnal self, but not to any great displeasure of them; but now he will please God, let flesh and self be never so much displeased. This is the great change that God will make upon all that shall be saved.

You can say, that the Holy Ghost is our sanctifier; but do you know what sanctification is? Why, this is what I have now opened to you; and every man and woman in the world must have this, or be condemned to everlasting misery. They must turn or die.

Do you believe all this, sirs, or do you not? Surely you dare not say you do not; for it is past a doubt or denial. These are not controversies, where one learned pious man is of one mind, and another of another; where one party saith this, and the other saith that. Every sect among us that deserve to be called Christians are all agreed in this that I have said; and if you will not believe the God of truth, and that in a case where every sect and party do believe him, you are utterly inexcusable.

But if you do believe this, how comes it to pass that you live so quietly in an unconverted state? Do you know that you are converted? and can you find this wonderful change upon your souls? Have you been

thus born again, and made new? Are not these
strange matters to many of you, and such as you
never felt within yourselves? If you cannot tell the
day or week of your change, or the very sermon that
converted you, yet do you find that the work is done,
that such a change indeed there is, and that you have
such hearts as are before described? Alas! the most
do follow their worldly business, and little trouble their
minds with such thoughts. And if they be restrained
from scandalous sins, and can say, " I am no whoremonger, nor thief, nor curser, nor swearer, nor tippler,
nor extortioner; I go to church, and say my prayers;"
they think that this is true conversion, and they shall
be saved as well as any. Alas! this is foolish cheat-
ing of yourselves. This is too much contempt of an
endless glory, and too gross neglect of your immortal
souls. Can you make so light of heaven and hell?
Your corpse will shortly lie in the dust, and angels or
devils will presently seize upon your souls; and every
man or woman of you all will shortly be among other
company, and in another case than now you are.
You will dwell in these houses but a little longer; you
will work in your shops and fields but a little longer;
you will sit in these seats and dwell on this earth but
a little longer; you will see with these eyes, and hear
with these ears, and speak with these tongues, but a
little longer, till the resurrection-day; and can you
make shift to forget this? O what a place will you
shortly be in of joy or torment! O what a sight will
you short.y see in heaven or hell! O what thoughts
will shortly fill your hearts with unspeakable delight
or horror! What work will you be employed in! to
praise the Lord with saints and angels, or to cry out
in fire unquenchable, with devils; and should all this

be forgotten? And all this will be endless, and sealed up by an unchangeable decree. Eternity, eternity will be the measure of your joys or sorrows: and can this be forgotten? And all this is true, sirs, most certainly true. When you have gone up and down a little longer, and slept and awaked a few times more, you will be dead and gone, and find all true that now I tell you: and yet can you now so much forget it? You shall then remember that you had this call, and that, this day, in this place, you were reminded of these things, and perceive them matters a thousand times greater than either you or I could here conceive; and yet shall they be now so much forgotten?

Beloved friends, if the Lord had not awakened me to believe and to lay to heart these things myself, I should have remained in a dark and selfish state, and have perished for ever; but if he have truly made me sensible of them, it will constrain me to compassionate you as well as myself. If your eyes were so far opened as to see hell, and you saw your neighbors that were unconverted dragged thither with hideous cries; though they were such as you accounted honest people on earth, and feared no such danger themselves, such a sight would make you go home and think of it, and think again, and make you warn all about you, as that lost worldling, Luke 16 : 28, would have had his brethren warned, lest they come to that place of torment. Why, faith is a kind of sight; it is the eye of the soul, the evidence of things not seen. If I believe God, it is next to seeing; and therefore I beseech you excuse me if I be half as earnest with you about these matters as if I had seen them. If I must die to-morrow, and it were in my power to come again from another world, and tell you what I had seen, would you not be willing to hear me? and would you not believe, and regard what I should tell you? If I might preach one sermon to you after I am dead, and have seen what is done in the world to come, would you not have me plainly speak the truth, and would you not crowd to hear me, and would you not lay it to heart? But this must not be; God hath his appointed way of teaching you by Scriptures and ministers, and he will not humor unbelievers so far as to send men from the dead to them, and alter his established way; if any man quarrel with the sun, God will not humor him so far as to set up a clearer light. Friends, I beseech you regard me now as you would do if I should come from the dead to you; for I can give you as full assurance of the truth of what I say to you as if I had been there and seen it with my eyes; for it is possible for one from the dead to deceive you; but Jesus Christ can never deceive you; the Word of God delivered in Scripture, and sealed by miracles, and holy workings of the Spirit, can never deceive you. Believe this or believe nothing. Believe and obey this, or you are undone. Now, as ever you believe the word of God, and as ever you care for the salvation of your souls, let me beg of you this reasonable request, and I beseech you deny me not: That you would now remember what has been said, and enter into an earnest search of your hearts, and say to yourselves—Is it so indeed; must I turn or die? Must I be converted or condemned? It is time for me then to look about me before it be too late. O why did not I look after this till now? Why did I venturously put off or neglect so great a business? Was I awake, or in my wits? O blessed God, what a mercy is it that thou didst not cut off my life all this while, be-

fore I had any certain hope of eternal life! Well,
God forbid that I should neglect this work any longer.
What state is my soul in? Am I converted, or am I
not? Was ever such a change or work done upon my
soul? Have I been illuminated by the word and
Spirit of the Lord to see the odiousness of sin, the
need of a Savior, the love of Christ, and the excel-
lences of God and glory? Is my heart broken or humbled within me for my former life? Have I thankfully entertained my Savior and Lord that offered
himself with pardon and life for my soul? Do I hate
my former sinful life and the remnant of every sin
that is in me? Do I fly from them as my deadly enemies? Do I give up myself to a life of holiness and
obedience to God? Do I love it and delight in it?
Can I truly say that I am dead to the world, and carnal self, and that I live for God and the glory which
he hath promised? Hath heaven more of my estimation and resolution than earth? And is God the
dearest and highest in my soul? Once, I am sure, I
lived principally to the world and flesh, and God had
nothing but some heartless services, which the world
could spare, and which were the leavings of the flesh.
Is my heart now turned another way? Have I a new
design and a new end, and a new train of holy affections? Have I set my hopes and heart in heaven?
And is it not the scope, and design, and bent of my
heart, to get well to heaven, and see the glorious face
of God, and live in his love and praise? And when
I sin, is it against the habitual bent and design of my
heart? And do I conquer all gross sins, and am I
weary and willing to be rid of my infirmities? This
is the state of converted souls. And thus it must be
with me, or I must perish. Is it thus with me indeed,

or is it not? It is time to get this doubt resolved, before the dreadful Judge resolve it. I am not such a stranger to my own heart and life, but I may somewhat perceive whether I am thus converted or not: if I be not, it will do me no good to flatter my soul with false conceits and hopes. I am resolved no more to deceive myself, but endeavor to know truly whether I be converted or not : that if I be, I may rejoice in it, and glorify my gracious Lord, and comfortably go on till I reach the crown : and if I am not, I may set myself to beg and seek after the grace that should convert me, and may turn without any more delay. For, if I find in time that I am out of the way, by the help of Christ I may turn and be recovered ; but if I stay till either my heart be forsaken of God in blindness or hardness, or till I be catched away by death, it is then too late. There is no place for repentance and conversion then; I know it must be now or never.

Sirs, this is my request to you, that you will but take your hearts to task, and thus examine them till you see, if it may be, whether you are converted or not? And if you cannot find it out by your own endeavors, go to your ministers, if they be faithful and experienced men, and desire their assistance. The matter is great; let not bashfulness, nor carelessness hinder you. They are set over you, to advise you, for the saving of your soul, as physicians advise you for the curing of your bodies. It undoes many thousands that they think they are in the way to salvation when they are not; and think that they are converted when it is no such thing. And then when we call to them daily to turn, they go away as they came, and think that this concerns not them; for they are turned already, and hope they shall do well enough in the way that they are in, at least if they pick the fairest path, and avoid some of the foulest steps, when, alas! all this while they live but to the world and flesh, and are strangers to God and eternal life; and are quite out of the way to heaven. And all this because we cannot persuade them to a few serious thoughts of their condition, and to spend a few hours in the examining of their states. Are there not many self-deceivers who hear me this day, that never bestowed one hour, or quarter of an hour, in all their lives, to examine their souls, and try whether they are truly converted or not? O merciful God, that will care for such wretches that care no more for themselves, and that will do so much to save them from hell, and help them to heaven, who will do so little for it themselves! If all that are in the way to hell, and in the state of damnation, did but know it, they durst not continue in it. The greatest hope that the devil hath of bringing you to damnation without a rescue, is by keeping you blindfold, and ignorant of your state, and making you believe that you may do well enough in the way that you are in. If you knew that you were out of the way to heaven, and were lost for ever if you should die as you are, durst you sleep another night in the state that you are in? Durst you live another day in it? Could you heartily laugh, or be merry in such a state? What! And not know but you may be snatched away to hell in an hour? Sure it would constrain you to forsake your former company and courses, and to betake yourselves to the ways of holiness and the communion of saints. Sure it would drive you to cry to God for a new heart, and to seek help of those that are fit to counsel you. There are none of you that care for being damned. Well, then I beseech you presently make inquiry into your hearts, and give them no rest till you find out your condition, that if it be good, you may rejoice in it, and go on; and if it be bad, you may presently look about you for recovery, as men that believe they must turn or die. What say you, sirs, will you resolve and promise to be at thus much labor for your own souls? Will you now enter upon this self-examination? Is my request unreasonable? Your consciences know it is not. Resolve on it then, before you stir; knowing how much it concerneth your souls. I beseech you, for the sake of that God that doth command you, at whose bar you will all shortly appear, that you do not deny me this reasonable request. For the sake of those souls that must turn or die, I beseech you deny me not; but make it your business to understand your own conditions, and build upon sure ground, and know whether you are converted or not; and venture not your souls on negligent security.

But perhaps you will say, ' What if we should find ourselves yet unconverted, what shall we do then?' This question leads me to my second Doctrine, which will do much to the answering of it, to which I now proceed.

DOCTRINE II

It is the promise of God, that the wicked shall live, if they will, but turn—unfeignedly and thoroughly turn.

.The Lord here professeth that this is what he takes pleasure in, that the wicked turn and live. Heaven is made as sure to the converted, as hell is to the unconverted. Turn and live, is as certain a truth as turn or die. God was not bound to provide us a Savior, nor open to us a door of hope, nor call us to repent and turn, when once we had cast ourselves away by sin. But he hath freely done it to magnify his mercy. Sinners, there are none of you shall have cause to go home, and say I preach desperation to you. Do we use to shut the door of mercy against you? O that you would not shut it up against yourselves! Do we use to tell you that God will have no mercy on you, though you turn and be sanctified? When did you ever hear a preacher say such a word? You that cavil at the preachers of the Gospel for desiring to keep you out of hell, and say, that they preach desperation; tell me if you can; when did you ever hear any sober man say, that there is no hope for you, though you repent, and be converted? No, it is the direct contrary that we daily proclaim from the Lord; and whoever is born again, and by faith and repentance doth become a new creature, shall certainly be saved; and so far are we from persuading you to despair of this, that we persuade you not to make any doubt of it. It is life, not death, that is the first part of our message to you; our commission is to offer salvation, certain salvation; a speedy, glorious, everlasting salvation, to every one of you; to the poorest beggar as well as the greatest lord; to the worst of you, even to drunkards, swearers, worldlings, thieves, yea, to the despisers and reproachers of the holy way of salvation. We are commanded by the Lord our Master to offer you a pardon for all that is past, if you will but now at last return and live; we are commanded to beseech and entreat you to accept the offer, and return; to tell you what preparation is made by Christ; what mercy stays for you; what patience waiteth for you; what thoughts of kindness God hath toward you; and how happy, how certainly and unspeakably happy you may be if you will. We have indeed also a message of wrath and death, yea, of a twofold wrath and death; but neither of them is our principal message. We must tell you of the wrath that is on you already, and the death that you are born under, for the breach of the law of works; but this is but to show you the need of mercy, and to provoke you to esteem the grace of the Redeemer. And we tell you nothing but the truth, which you must know; for who will seek for physic that knows not that he is sick? Our telling you of your misery is not that which makes you miserable, but driveth you out to seek for mercy. It is you that have brought this death upon yourselves. We tell you also of another death, even remediless, and much greater torment, that will fall on those that will not be converted. But as this is true, and must be told you, so it is but the last and saddest part of our message. We are first to offer you mercy, if you will turn; and it is only those that will not turn, nor hear the voice of mercy, to whom we must foretell damnation. Will you but cast away your transgressions, delay no longer, but come away at the call of Christ, and be converted, and become new creatures, and we have not a word of damning wrath or death to speak against you. I do here, in the name of the Lord of Life, proclaim to you all that hear me this day, to the worst of you, to the greatest, to the oldest sinner, that you may have mercy and salvation, if you will but turn. There is mercy in God, there is sufficiency in the satisfaction of Christ, the promise is free, and full, and universal; you may have life, if you will but turn. But then,

as you love your souls, remember what turning it is
that the Scripture speaks of. It is not to mend the old
house, but to pull down all, and build anew on Christ,
the Rock, and sure foundation. It is not to mend
somewhat in a carnal course of life, but to mortify the
flesh, and live after the Spirit. It is not to serve the
flesh and the world, in a more reformed way, without
any scandalous disgraceful sins, and with a certain
kind of religiousness; but it is to change your master,
and your works, and end; and to set your face the
contrary way, and do all for the life that you never
saw, and dedicate yourselves and all you have to
God. This is the change that must be made, if you
will live.

Yourselves are witnesses now, that it is salvation,
and not damnation, that is the great doctrine I preach
to you, and the first part of my message to you. Accept of this, and we shall go no farther with you;
for we would not so much as affright, or trouble you
with the name of damnation, without necessity.

But if you will not be saved, there is no remedy,
but damnation must take place; for there is no middle
place between the two; you must have either life or
death.

And we are not only to offer you life, but to show
you the grounds on which we do it, and call you to
believe that God doth mean, indeed, as he speaks;
that the promise is true, and extended conditionally
to you, as well as others; and that heaven is no fancy,
but a true felicity.

If you ask, Where is your commission for this offer?
Among a hundred texts of Scripture, I will show it to
you in these few:

First, You see it here in my text, and the following

verses, and in the 18th of Ezekiel, as plain as can be
spoken; and in 2 Cor. 5 : 17, 21, you have the very
sum of our commission : " If any man be in Christ, he
is a new creature: old things are passed away; behold, all things are become new. And all things are
of God, who hath reconciled us to himself by Jesus
Christ, and hath given to us the ministry of reconci-
liation; to wit, that God was in Christ reconciling the
world unto himself, not imputing their trespasses to
them, and hath committed unto us the word of recon-
ciliation.   Now then, we are ambassadors for Christ,
as though God did beseech you by us : we pray you
in Christ's stead, be ye reconciled unto God.   For he
hath made him to be sin for us, who knew no sin; that
we might be made the righteousness of God in him."
So Mark, 16 : 15, 16, " Go ye into all the world, and
preach the Gospel to every creature.   He that believeth," (that is with such a converting faith as is ex-
pressed,) " and is baptized, shall be saved; and he
that believeth not, shall be damned."   And Luke,
24 : 46, 47 : " Thus it behoved Christ to suffer, and
to rise from the dead the third day : and that repentance" (which is conversion) " and remission of sins
should be preached in his name among all nations."
And, Acts 5 : 30, 31, " The God of our fathers raised
up Jesus, whom ye slew, and hanged on a tree: him
hath God exalted with his right hand, to be a Prince
and a Savior, to give repentance to Israel, and forgiveness of sins."   And Acts, 13 : 38, 39, " Be it known
unto you, therefore, men and brethren, that through
this man is preached unto you the forgiveness of sins;
and by him all that believe are justified from all
things, from which ye could not be justified by the
law of Moses."   And lest you think this offer is re-

strained to the Jews, see Gal. 6 : 15, " For in Christ Jesus, neither circumcision availeth any thing, nor uncircumcision, but a new creature." And Luke, 14 : 17, " Come, for all things are now ready."

You see by this time that we are commanded to offer life to you all, and to tell you from God, that if you will turn, you may live.

Here you may safely trust your souls; for the love of God is the foundation of this offer, (John, 3 : 16,) and the blood of the Son of God hath purchased it ; the faithfulness and truth of God is engaged to make the promise good; miracles oft sealed the truth of it ; preachers are sent through the world to proclaim it ; and the Spirit doth open the heart to entertain it, and is itself the earnest of the full possession : so that the truth of it is past controversy, that the worst of you all, and every one of you, if you will but be converted, may be saved.

Indeed, if you will believe that you shall be saved without conversion, then you believe a falsehood ; and if I should preach that to you, I should preach a lie. This were not to believe God, but the devil and your own deceitful hearts. God hath his promise of life, and the devil hath his promise of life. God's promise is, Return and live. The devil's promise is, You shall live whether you turn or not. The words of God are, as I have showed you, " Except ye be converted and become as little children, ye cannot enter into the kingdom of heaven." Matt. 18 : 3. " Except a man be born again, he cannot enter into the kingdom of God." John, 3 : 3, 5. " Without holiness no man shall see the Lord." Heb. 12 : 14. The devil's word is, " You may be saved without being born again and converted ; you may do well enough without being

holy, God doth but frighten you; he is more merciful
than to do as he saith, he will be better to you than
his word." And, alas, the greatest part of the world
believe this word of the devil before the word of God;
just as our sin and misery came into the world. God
said to our first parents, "If ye eat ye shall die;" and
the devil contradicted him, and said, "Ye shall not
die:" and the woman believed the devil before God.
So now the Lord saith, Turn or die: and the devil
saith, You shall not die, if you do but cry for God's
mercy at last, and give over the acts of sin when you
can practise it no longer. And this is the word that
the world believes. O heinous wickedness, to believe
the devil before God.

And yet that is not the worst; but blasphemously
they call this a believing and trusting in God, when
they put him in the shape of satan, who was a liar
from the beginning; and when they believe that the
word of God is a lie, they call this a trusting God, and
say they believe in him, and trust in him for salvation. Where did ever God say, that the unregenerate,
unconverted, unsanctified, shall be saved? Show me
such a word in Scripture. Why this is the devil's
word, and to believe it is to believe the devil, and the
sin that is commonly called presumption; and do you
call this a believing and trusting in God? There is
enough in the word of God to comfort and strengthen
the heart of the sanctified, but not a word to strengthen
the hands of wickedness, nor to give men the least hope
of being saved though they be never sanctified.

But if you will turn, and come into the way of
mercy, the mercy of the Lord is ready to entertain
you. Then trust God for salvation, boldly and confi-
dently; for he is engaged by his word to save you.

He will be a father to none but his children; and he will save none but those that forsake the world, the devil, and the flesh, and come into his family to be members of his Son, and have communion with his saints. But if they will not come in, it is the fault of themselves: his doors are open; he keeps none back; he never sent such a message as this to any of you, " It is now too late; I will not receive thee, though thou be converted." He might have done so and done you no wrong; but he did not; he doth not to this day. He is still ready to receive you, if you were but ready unfeignedly, and with all your hearts, to turn. And the fulness of this truth will yet more appear in the two following doctrines, which I shall therefore next proceed to before I make any further application of this.

DOCTRINE III

*God taketh pleasure in men's conversion and sal-
vation, but not in their death or damnation He
had rather they would turn and live, than go on
and die.*

" The Lord is long suffering to us-ward," says the apostle, " not willing that any should perish, but that all should come to repentance." 2 Pet. 3 : 9. He un-feignedly willeth the conversion of all men, even of those that never will be converted, but not as absolute Lord with the fullest efficacious resolution, nor as a thing which he resolveth shall undoubtedly come to pass, or would engage all his power to accomplish. It is in the power of a prince to set a guard upon a murderer, to see that he shall not murder, and be hanged; but if, upon good reason, he forbear this, and do but send to his subjects to warn and entreat them not to be murderers, he may well say that he would not have them murder and be hanged; he takes no pleasure in it, but rather that they forbear and live, and if he do more for some upon some special reason, he is not bound to do so by all. The king may well say to all murderers and felons in the land, " I have no pleasure in your death, but rather that you would obey my laws and live; but if you will not, I am resolved, for all this, that you shall die." The judge may truly say to the murderer, " Alas, I have no delight in thy death; I had rather thou hadst kept the law and saved thy life; but seeing thou hast not, I must condemn thee, or else I should be unjust." So, though God have no pleasure in your damnation, and therefore calls upon you to return and live, yet he hath pleasure in the demonstration of his own justice, and the executing of his laws; and therefore he is, for all this, fully resolved, that if you will not be converted, you shall be condemned. If God was so much against the death of the wicked as that he were resolved to do all that he can to hinder it, then no man should be condemned; whereas Christ telleth you, that " narrow is the way that leadeth unto life, and few there be that find it." But so far God is opposed to your damnation as that he will teach you, and warn you, and set before you life and death, and offer you your choice, and command his ministers to entreat you not to destroy yourselves, but accept his mercy, and so to leave you without excuse. But if this will not do, and if still you be unconverted, he professeth to you, he is resolved on your damnation, and hath commanded us to say to you in his name, verse 8, " O wicked man thou shalt surely die!" And Christ hath little less than sworn it, over and over, with a " verily, verily, except ye be converted and born again, ye cannot enter into the kingdom of heaven." Matt. 18 : 3.   John, 3 : 3.   Mark, that he saith, " you cannot." It is in vain to hope for it, and in vain to dream that God is willing for it; for it is a thing that cannot be.

In a word, you see then the meaning of the text, that God, the great Lawgiver of the world, doth take no pleasure in the death of the wicked, but rather that they turn and live; though yet he be resolved that none shall live but those that turn; and as a judge, even delighteth in justice, and in manifesting his hatred of sin, though not in the misery which sinners have brought upon themselves, in itself considered.

And for the proofs of the point, I shall be very brief in them, because I suppose you easily believe it already.

1. The very gracious nature of God proclaimed · " And the Lord passed by before him, and proclaimed, The Lord, the Lord God, merciful and gracious, long-suffering, and abundant in goodness and truth, keeping mercy for thousands, forgiving iniquity, and transgression, and sin, and that will by no means clear the guilty;" (Exod. 34 : 6, 7;) and frequently elsewhere, may assure you of this, That he hath no pleasure in your death.

2. If God had more pleasure in thy death, than in thy conversion and life, he would not have so frequently commanded thee in his word, to turn; he would not have made thee such promises of life, if thou wilt but turn: he would not have persuaded thee to it by so many reasons. The tenor of his Gospel proveth the point.

3. And his commission that he hath given to the ministers of the Gospel doth fully prove it. If God had taken more pleasure in thy damnation, than in thy conversion and salvation, he would never have charged us to offer you mercy, and to teach you the way of life, both publicly and privately : and to entreat and beseech you to turn and live ; to acquaint you with your sins, and foretell you of your danger ; and to do all that possibly we can for your conversion, and to continue patiently so doing, though you should hate or abuse us for our pains. Would God have done this, and appointed his ordinances for your good, if he had taken pleasure in your death ?

4. It is proved also by the course of his providence. If God had rather you were damned than converted and saved, he would not second his word with his works, and entice you by his daily kindness to himself, and give you all the mercies of this life, which are means " to lead you to repentance," (Rom. 2 : 4,) and bring you so often under his rod, to lead you to your senses ; he would not set so many examples before your eyes, no, nor wait on you so patiently as he does from day to day, and year to year. These are not signs of one that taketh pleasure in your death. If this had been his delight, how easily could he have had thee long ago in hell ? How oft, before this, could he have catched thee away in the midst of thy sins with a curse or oath, or lie in thy mouth, in thy ignorance, and pride, and sensuality ? When thou wert last in thy drunkenness, or last deriding the ways of God, how easily could he have stopped thy breath, and tamed thee with plagues, and made thee sober in another world ! Alas ! how small a matter is it for the Almighty to rule the tongue of the profanest railer,

and tie the hands of the most malicious persecutor, or
calm the fury of the bitterest of his enemies, and make
them know that they are but worms? If he should
but frown upon thee thou wouldst drop into thy grave
If he gave commission to one of his angels to go and
destroy ten thousand sinners, how quickly would it be
done! how easily can he lay thee upon the bed of
languishing, and make thee lie roaring there in pain,
and make thee eat the words of reproach which thou
hast spoken against his servants, his word, his worship, and his holy ways, and make thee send to beg
their prayers whom thou didst despise in thy presumption? How easily can he lay that flesh under pains,
and groans, and make it too weak to hold thy soul,
and make it more loathsome than the dung of the
earth? That flesh which now must have what it
loves, and must not be displeased, though God be displeased; and must be humored in meat, and drink,
and clothes, whatever God say to the contrary, how
quickly would the frowns of God consume it? When
thou wast passionately defending thy sin, and quarrelling with them that would have drawn thee from
it, and showing thy spleen against the reprover, and
pleading for the works of darkness; how easily could
God have snatched thee away in a moment, and set
thee before his dreadful Majesty, where thou shouldst
see ten thousand times ten thousand glorious angels
waiting on his throne, and have called thee there to
plead thy cause, and asked thee " What hast thou
now to say against thy Creator, his truth, his servants,
or his holy ways? Now plead thy cause, and make
the best of it thou canst. Now what canst thou say
in excuse of thy sins? Now give account of thy world
liness and fleshly life, of thy time, of all the mercies

thou hast had." O how thy stubborn heart would
have melted, and thy proud looks be taken down, and
thy countenance be appalled, and thy stout words
turned into speechless silence, or dreadful cries, if God
had but set thee thus at his bar, and pleaded his own
cause with thee, which thou hast here so maliciously
pleaded against! How easily can he at any time say
to thy guilty soul, Come away, and live in that flesh
no more till the resurrection, and it cannot resist! A
word of his mouth would take off the poise of thy present life, and then all thy parts and powers would
stand still; and if he say unto thee, Live no longer, or,
live in hell, thou couldst not disobey.

But God hath yet done none of this, but hath patiently forborne thee, and mercifully upheld thee, and
given thee that breath which thou didst breathe out
against him, and given those mercies which thou
didst sacrifice to thy flesh, and afforded thee that provision which thou didst use to satisfy thy greedy
throat: he gave thee every minute of that time which
thou didst waste in idleness, or drunkenness, or worldliness; and doth not all his patience and mercy show
that he desired not thy damnation? Can the candle
burn without the oil? Can your houses stand without
the earth to bear them? No more can you live an
hour without the support of God. And why did he
so long support thy life, but to see when thou wouldst
bethink thee of the folly of thy ways, and return and
live? Will any man purposely put arms into his enemy's hands to resist him, or hold a candle to a murderer that is killing his children, or to an idle servant
that plays or sleeps the while? Surely it is to see
whether thou wilt at last return and live, that God
hath so long waited on thee.

5. It is further proved by the suffering of his Son,
that God taketh no pleasure in the death of the wicked.
Would he have ransomed them from death at so dear
a rate? Would he have astonished angels and men
by his condescension? Would God have dwelt in
flesh, and have come in the form of a servant, and
have assumed humanity into one person with the God-
head; and would Christ have lived a life of suffering,
and died a cursed death for sinners, if he had rather
taken pleasure in their death? Suppose you saw him
but so busy in preaching and healing of them, as you
find him in Mark, 3 : 21; or so long in fasting, as in
Matt. 4; or all night in prayer, as in Luke 6 : 12; or
praying with the drops of blood trickling from him
instead of sweat, as Luke 22 : 44; or suffering a cursed
death upon the cross, and pouring out his soul as a sacrifice for our sins—would you have thought these the
signs of one that delighted in the death of the wicked?

And think not to extenuate it by saying, that it
was only for his elect : for it was thy sin, and the sin
of all the world, that lay upon our Redeemer; and his
sacrifice and satisfaction is sufficient for all, and the
fruits of it are offered to one as well as another. But it
is true, that it was never the intent of his mind to pardon and save any that would not, by faith and repentance, be converted. If you had seen and heard him
weeping and bemoaning the state of disobedience in
impenitent people : (Luke, 19 · 41, 42,) " And when
he was come near, he beheld the city, and wept over
it, saying, if thou hadst known, even thou, at least in
this thy day, the things which belong unto thy peace !
but now they are hid from thine eyes"—or complain-
ing of their stubbornness, as Matt. 23 : 37, " O Jerusalem, Jerusalem, how often would I have gathered

thy children together, even as a hen gathereth her chickens under her wings, and ye would not !" or if you had seen and heard him on the cross, praying for his persecutors—Father, forgive them, for they know not what they do—would you have suspected that he had delighted in the death of the wicked, even of those that perish by their wilful unbelief? When God hath so loved, (not only loved, but so loved,) as to give his only begotten Son, that whosoever believeth in him (by an effectual faith) should not perish, but have everlasting life, I think he hath hereby proved, against the malice of men and devils, that he takes no pleasure in the death of the wicked, but had rather that they would " turn and live."

6. Lastly, If all this will not yet satisfy you, take His own word that knoweth best his own mind, or at least believe his oath : but this leads me to the fourth doctrine.

DOCTRINE IV

The Lord hath confirmed to us by his Oath, that he hath no pleasure in the death of the wicked, but rather that he turn and live; that he may leave man no pretence to question the truth of it.

If you dare question his word, I hope you dare not question his oath. As Christ hath solemnly protested that the unregenerate and unconverted cannot enter into the kingdom of heaven; (Matt. 18 : 3; John, 3 : 3;) so God hath sworn that his pleasure is not in their death, but in their conversion and life. And as the apostle saith, (Heb. 4 : 13, 18,) because he can swear by no greater, he sware by himself. " For men verily swear by the greater : and an oath for confirma-

tion is to them an end of strife. Wherein God, willing more abundantly to show unto the heirs of promise the immutability of his counsel, confirmed it by
an oath; that by two immutable things in which it
was impossible for God to lie, we might have strong
consolation, who have fled for refuge to lay hold on
the hope set before us: which hope we have as an
anchor of the soul both sure and steadfast." If there
be any man that cannot reconcile this truth with the
doctrine of predestination, or the actual damnation of
the wicked, that is his own ignorance; he hath no
pretence left to question or deny therefore the truth of
the point in hand; for this is confirmed by the oath
of God, and therefore must not be distorted, to reduce
it to other points: but doubtful points must rather be
reduced to it, and certain truths must be believed to
agree with it, though our shallow minds hardly discern the agreement.

USE.—I do now entreat thee, if thou be an unconverted sinner that hearest these words, that thou
wouldst ponder a little upon the forementioned doctrines, and bethink thyself awhile who it is that takes
pleasure in thy sin and damnation. Certainly it is
not God; he hath sworn for his part that he takes no
pleasure in it. And I know it is not the pleasing of
him that you intend. You dare not say that you
drink, and swear, and neglect holy duties, and quench
the motions of the Spirit to please God. That were
as if you should reproach the prince, and break his
laws, and seek his death, and say you did all this to
please him.

Who is it then that takes pleasure in your sin and
death? Not any that bear the image of God, for they

must be like minded to him. God knows, it is small pleasure to your faithful teachers to see you serve your deadly enemy, and madly venture your eternal state, and wilfully run into the flames of hell. It is small pleasure to them to see upon your souls (in the sad effects) such blindness, and hard-heartedness, and carelessness, and presumption; such wilfulness in evil, and such unteachableness and stiffness against the ways of life and peace; they know these are marks of death, and of the wrath of God, and they know, from the word of God, what is like to be the end of them, and therefore it is no more pleasure to them than to a tender physician to see the plague-marks broke out upon his patient. Alas, to foresee your everlasting torments, and know not how to prevent them! To see how near you are to hell, and we cannot make you believe it and consider it. To see how easily, how certainly you might escape, if we knew but how to make you willing. How fair you are for everlasting salvation, if you would turn and do your best, and make it the care and business of your lives! but you will not do it; if our lives lay on it, we cannot persuade you to it. We study day and night what to say to you that may convince and persuade you, and yet it is undone: we lay before you the word of God, and show you the very chapter and verse where it is written, that you cannot be saved except you be converted; and yet we leave the most of you as we find you. We hope you will believe the word of God, though you believe not us, and regard it when we show you the plain Scripture for it; but we hope in vain, and labor in vain as to any saving change upon your hearts! And do you think that this is a pleasant thing to us? Many a time, in secret prayer, we are

fain to complain to God with sad hearts, " Alas, Lord,
we have spoken to them in thy name, but they little
regard us; we have told them what thou bidst us tell
them concerning the danger of an unconverted state,
but they do not believe us: we have told them that
thou hast protested that there is no peace to the
wicked;" (Isa. 57 : 21;) " but the worst of them all
will scarcely believe that they are wicked. We
have showed them thy word, where thou hast said,
that if they live after the flesh they shall die;" (Rom.
8 : 13,) " but they say, they will believe in thee, when
they will not believe thee; and that they will trust in
thee, when they give no credit to thy word; and when
they hope that the threatenings of thy word are false,
they will yet call this a hoping in God; and though
we show them where thou hast said, that when a
wicked man dieth, all his hopes perish, yet cannot we
persuade them from their deceitful hopes." Prov.
11 : 7. " We tell them what a base unprofitable
thing sin is; but they love it, and therefore will not
leave it. We tell them how dear they buy this pleasure, and what they must pay for it in everlasting
torment; and they bless themselves, and will not believe it, but will do as the most do; and because God
is merciful, they will not believe him, but will venture their souls, come what will. We tell them how
ready the Lord is to receive them, and this doth but
make them delay their repentance and be bolder in
their sin. Some of them say they purpose to repent,
but they are still the same; and some say they do repent already, while yet they are not converted from
their sins. We exhort them, we entreat them, we
offer them our help, but we cannot prevail with them
but they that were drunkards, are drunkards still; and

they that were voluptuous flesh-pleasing wretches, are such still; and they that were worldlings, are worldlings still; and they that were ignorant, and proud, and self-conceited, are so still. Few of them will see and confess their sin, and fewer will forsake it, but comfort themselves that all men are sinners, as if there were no difference between a converted sinner and an unconverted. Some of them will not come near us, when we are willing to instruct them, but think they know enough already, and need not our instruction; and some of them will give us the hearing, and do what they list; and most of them are like dead men that cannot feel; so that when we tell them of the matters of everlasting consequence, we cannot get a word of it to their hearts. If we do not obey them, and humor them in doing all that they would have us, though never so much against the word of God, they will hate us, and rail at us; but if we beseech them to confess, and forsake their sins, and save their souls, they will not do it. They would have us disobey God and damn our own souls, to please them; and yet they will not turn and save their own souls to please God. They are wiser in their own eyes than all their teachers; they rage and are confident in their own way, and if we are ever so anxious we cannot change them. Lord, this is the case of our miserable neighbors, and we cannot help it; we see them ready to drop into hell, and we cannot help it; we know if they would unfeignedly turn, they might be saved, but we cannot persuade them; if we would beg it of them on our knees, we cannot persuade them to it; if we would beg it of them with tears, we cannot persuade them; and what more can we do?

These are the secret complaints and moans that

many a poor minister is compelled to make. And do you think that he hath any pleasure in this? Is it a pleasure to him to see you go on in sin, and cannot stop you? to see you so miserable, and cannot so much as make you sensible of it? to see you merry when you are not sure to be an hour out of hell? to think what you must for ever suffer, because you will not turn? and to think what an everlasting life of glory you wilfully despise and cast away? What sadder thing can you bring to their hearts, and how can you devise to grieve them more?

Who is it then that you please by your sin and death? It is none of your understanding godly friends. Alas, it is the grief of their souls to see your misery, and they lament you many a time when you give them little thanks for it, and when you have not hearts to lament yourselves.

Who is it then that takes pleasure in your sin?

1. The devil indeed takes pleasure in your sin and death; for this is the very end of all his temptations; for this he watches night and day; you cannot devise to please him better than to go on in sin. How glad is he when he sees thee going into the alehouse, or other sin, and when he heareth thee curse, or swear, or rail? How glad is he when he heareth thee revile the minister that would draw thee from thy sin, and help to save thee? These are his delight.

2. The wicked are also delighted in it; for it is agreeable to their nature.

3. But I know, for all this, that it is not the pleasing of the devil that you intend, even when you please him; but it is your own flesh, the greatest and most dangerous enemy, that you intend to please. It is the flesh that would be pampered, that would be pleased

in meat, and drink, and clothing; that would be pleased in your company, and pleased in applause and credit with the world, and pleased in sports, and lusts, and idleness; this is the gulf that devoureth all. This is the very god that you serve, for the Scripture saith of such, that their bellies are their gods. Phil. **3** : **19.** But I beseech you stay a little and consider the business.

1. *Question.* Should your flesh be pleased before your maker ? Will you displease the Lord, and displease your teacher, and your godly friends, and all to please your brutish appetites, or sensual desires? Is not God worthy to be the ruler of your flesh ? If he shall not rule it, he will not save it; you cannot in reason expect that he should.

2. *Question.* Your flesh is pleased with your sin, but is your conscience pleased ? Doth not it grudge within you, and tell you sometimes that all is not well, and that your case is not so safe as you make it to be ; and should not your souls and consciences be pleased before your corruptible flesh ?

3. *Question.* But is not your flesh preparing for its own displeasure also ? It loves the bait, but doth it love the hook ? It loves the strong drink and sweet morsels ; it loves its ease, and sports, and merriment ; it loves to be rich, and well spoken of by men, and to be somebody in the world; but doth it love the curse of God ? Doth it love to stand trembling before his bar, and to be judged to everlasting fire? Doth it love to be tormented with the devils for ever ? Take all together ; for there is no separating sin and hell, but only by faith and true conversion ; if you will keep one, you must have the other. If death and hell be pleasant to thee, no wonder then if you go on in sin.

but if they be not, (as I am sure they are not,) then what if sin were never so pleasant, is it worth the loss of life eternal? Is a little drink, or meat, or ease; is the good word of sinners, is the riches of this world to be valued above the joys of heaven? Or are they worth the sufferings of eternal fire? Sirs, these questions should be considered before you go any further, by every man that hath reason to consider, and that believes he hath a soul to save or lose.

Well, the Lord here sweareth that he hath no pleasure in your death, but rather that you would turn and live; if yet you will go on and die rather than turn, remember it was not to please God that you did it: it was to please the world, and to please yourselves. And if men will damn themselves to please themselves, and run into endless torments for delight, and have not the wit, the hearts, the grace, to hearken to God or man that would reclaim them, what remedy is there, but they must take what they get by it, and repent it in another manner, when it is too late? Before I proceed any further in the application I shall come to the next doctrine, which gives me a fuller ground for it.

DOCTRINE V

So earnest is God for the conversion of sinners that he doubleth his commands and exhortations, with vehemency—Turn ye, turn ye, why will you die?

This doctrine is the application of the former, as by a use of exhortation, and accordingly I shall handle it. Is there an unconverted sinner that heareth these vehement words of God? Is there a man or woman in this assembly that is yet a stranger to the renewing sanctifying work of the Holy Ghost? It is a happy assembly, if it be not so with the most. Hearken then to the voice of your Maker, and turn to him by Christ without delay. Would you know the will of God? Why this is his will, that you presently turn. Shall the living God send so earnest a message to his creatures, and should they not obey?

Hearken then, all you that live after the flesh: the Lord that gave thee thy breath and being hath sent a message to thee from heaven; and this is his message, *Turn ye, turn ye, why will ye die?* He that hath ears to hear, let him hear. Shall the voice of the eternal Majesty be neglected? If he do but terribly thunder, thou art afraid. O but this voice doth more nearly concern thee. If he did but tell thee thou shalt die to-morrow, thou wouldst not make light of it. O but this word concerneth thy life or death everlasting. It is both a command and an exhortation. As if he had said to thee, "I charge thee, upon the allegiance that thou owest to me thy Creator and Redeemer, that thou renounce the flesh, the world, and the devil, and turn to me, that thou mayest live. I condescend to entreat thee, as thou either lovest or fearest him that made thee; as thou lovest thine own life, even thine everlasting life, turn and live: as ever thou wouldst escape eternal misery, turn, turn, for why wilt thou die?" And is there a heart in man, in a reasonable creature, that can once refuse such a message, such a command, such an exhortation as this? O what a thing, then, is the heart of man!

Hearken, then, all that love yourselves, and all that regard your own salvation; here is the most joyful message that was ever sent to the ears of man, " *Turn ye, turn ye, why will ye die?*" You are not yet shut up under desperation. Here is mercy offered you; turn, and you shall have it. O Sirs! with what glad and joyful hearts should you receive these tidings! I know this is not the first time that you have heard it; but how have you regarded it, or how do you regard it now? Hear, all you ignorant, careless sinners, the word of the Lord. Hear, all you worldlings, you sensual flesh-pleasers; you gluttons, and drunkards, and whoremongers, and swearers; you railers and backbiters, slanderers and liars—*Turn ye, turn ye, why will ye die?*

Hear, all you cold and outside professors, and all that are strangers to the life of Christ, and never knew the power of his cross and resurrection, and never felt your hearts warmed with his love, and live not on him as the strength of your souls—" Turn ye, turn ye, why will ye die?"

Hear, all that are void of the love of God, whose hearts are not toward him, nor taken up with the hopes of glory, but set more by your earthly prosperity and delights than by the joys of heaven; all you that are religious but a little-by-the-by, and give God no more than your flesh can spare; that have not denied your carnal selves, and forsaken all that you have for Christ, in the estimation and grounded resolution of your souls, but have some one thing in the world so dear to you that you cannot spare it for Christ, if he required it, but will rather venture on his displeasure than forsake it—" Turn ye, turn ye, why will ye die?"

If you never heard it, or observed it before, remember that you were told from the word of God this day, that if you will but turn, you may live; and if you will not turn, you shall surely die.

What now will you do, sirs? What is your resolution? Will you turn, or will you not? Halt not any longer between two opinions. If the Lord be God, follow him: if your flesh be God, then serve it still. If heaven be better than earth and fleshly pleasures, come away, then, and seek a better country, and lay up your treasure where rust and moths do not corrupt, and thieves cannot break through and steal; and be awakened at last, with all your might, to seek the kingdom that cannot be moved, (Heb. 12 : 28,) and to employ your lives on a higher design, and turn the stream of your cares and labors another way than formerly you have done. But if earth be better than heaven, or will do more for you, or last you longer, then keep it, and make your best of it, and follow it still. Sirs, are you resolved what to do? If you be not, I will set a few more moving considerations before you, to see if reason will make you resolve.

Consider, I. What preparations mercy hath made for your salvation; and what pity it is that any man should be damned after all this. The time was, when the flaming sword was in the way, and the curse of God's law would have kept thee back if thou hadst been never so willing to turn to God. The time was when thyself, and all the friends that thou hast in the world, could never have produced thee the pardon of thy sins past, though thou hadst never so much lamented and reformed them. But Christ hath removed this impediment, by the ransom of his blood. The time was, that God was wholly unreconciled, as being not satisfied for the violation of his law; but now he is so far satisfied and reconciled, as that he hath made thee a free act of oblivion, and a free deed of gift of Christ and life, and offereth it to thee, and en-

treateth thee to accept it ; and it may be thine, if thou
wilt. For, " he was in Christ reconciling the world
to himself, and hath committed to us the word of re-
conciliation." 2 Cor. 5 : 18, 19. Sinners, we too are
commanded to deliver this message to you all, as from
the Lord ; " Come, for all things are ready." Luke,
14 : 17. Are all things ready, and are you unready ?
God is ready to entertain you, and pardon all that
you have done against him, if you will but come. As
long as you have sinned, as wilfully as you have sinned, he is ready to cast all behind his back, if you
will but come. Though you have been prodigals,
and run away from God, and have staid so long, he
is ready even to meet you, and embrace you in his
arms, and rejoice in your conversion, if you will but
turn. Even the worldlings and drunkards will find
God ready to bid them welcome, if they will but come.
Doth not this turn thy heart within thee ? O sinner !
if thou hast a heart of flesh, and not of stone in thee,
methinks this should melt it. Shall the dreadful infinite Majesty of heaven even wait for thy returning,
and be ready to receive thee, who hast abused him,
and forgotten him so long ? Shall he delight in thy
conversion, that might at any time glorify his justice
in thy damnation ? and yet doth it not melt thy heart
within thee, and art thou not yet ready to come in ?
Hast thou not as much reason to be ready to come as
God hath to invite thee and bid thee welcome ?

But that is not all : Christ hath died on the cross,
and made such way for thee to the Father, that, on
his account, thou mayest be welcome, if thou wilt
come. And yet art thou not ready ?

A pardon is already expressly granted, and offered
thee in the Gospel. And yet art thou not ready ?

The ministers of the Gospel are ready to assist thee, to instruct thee, pray for thee. And yet art thou not ready?

All that fear God about thee are ready to rejoice in thy conversion, and to receive thee into the communion of saints, and to give thee the right hand of fellowship, yea, though thou hadst been one that had been cast out of their society : they dare not but forgive where God forgiveth, when it is manifest to them, by thy confession and amendment ; they dare not so much as reproach thee with thy former sins, because they know that God will not upbraid thee with them. If thou hadst been never so scandalous, if thou wouldst but heartily be converted and come in, they would not refuse thee, let the world say what they would against it. And are all these ready to receive thee, and yet art thou not ready to come in?

Yea, heaven itself is ready : The Lord will receive thee into the glory of his saints. Vile as thou hast been, if thou wilt be but cleansed thou mayest have a place before his throne ; his angels will be ready to guard thy soul to the place of joy if thou do but unfeignedly come in. And is God ready, the sacrifice of Christ ready, the promise ready, and pardon ready ? are ministers ready, and the people of God ready, and heaven itself ready ? and angels ready ? and all these but waiting for thy conversion ; and yet art thou not ready? What! not ready to live, when thou hast been dead so long? not ready to come to thy right understanding, as the prodigal is said to " come to himself," (Luke, 15 : 17,) when thou hast been beside thyself so long? Not ready to be saved, when thou art even ready to be condemned ? Art thou not ready to lay hold on Christ, that would deliver thee, when

thou art even ready to sink into damnation? Art thou
not ready to be drawn from hell, when thou art even
ready to be cast remediless into it? Alas, man! dost
thou know what thou doest? If thou die unconverted
there is no doubt to be made of thy damnation; and
thou art not sure to live an hour. And yet art thou
not ready to turn and to come in? O miserable
wretch! Hast thou not served the flesh and the devil
long enough? Yet hast thou not enough of sin? Is
it so good to thee, or so profitable for thee? Dost thou
know what it is, that thou wouldst yet have more of
it? Hast thou had so many calls, and so many mercies, and so many warnings, and so many examples?
Hast thou seen so many laid in the grave, and yet
art thou not ready to let go thy sins, and come to
Christ? What! after so many convictions and pangs
of conscience, after so many purposes and promises,
art thou not yet ready to turn and live? O that thy
eyes, thy heart, were opened to know how fair an offer
is now made to thee! and what a joyful message it is
that we are sent on, to bid thee come, for all things
are ready!

II. Consider also, what calls thou hast to turn and
live. How many, how loud, how earnest, how dreadful: and yet what encouraging, joyful calls! For the
principal inviter is God himself. He that commandeth heaven and earth, commands thee to turn, and
that presently, without delay. He commands the
sun to run its course, and to rise upon thee every
morning; and though it be so glorious an orb, and
many times bigger than all the earth, yet it obeyeth
him, and faileth not one minute of its appointed time.
He commandeth all the planets, and the orbs of heaven, and they obey. He commandeth the sea to ebb

and flow, and the whole creation to keep its course, and all obey him ; the angels of heaven obey his will, when he sends them to minister to such worms as we on earth, (Heb. 1 : 14;) and yet if he command but a sinner to turn, he will not obey him. He only thinks himself wiser than God, and he cavils and pleads the cause of sin, and will not obey. If the Lord Almighty say the word, the heavens and all therein obey him : but if he call but a drunkard out of an ale-house, he will not obey : or if he call a worldly fleshly sinner to deny himself, and mortify the flesh, and set his heart upon a better inheritance, he will not obey.

If thou hadst any love in thee, thou wouldst know the voice, and say, O this is my Father's call ! how can I find in my heart to disobey ? For the sheep of Christ " know and hear his voice, and they follow him, and he giveth them eternal life," John, 10 : 4. If thou hadst any spiritual life and sense in thee, at least thou wouldst say, " This call is the dreadful voice of God, and who dare disobey ? For saith the prophet, (Amos, 3 : 8,) " The lion hath roared, who will not fear ?" God is not a man, that thou shouldst dally and trifle with him. Remember what he said to Paul at his conversion, " *It is hard for thee to kick against the pricks.*" Acts, 9 : 5. Wilt thou yet go on and despise his word, and resist his Spirit, and stop thine ear against his call ? who is it that will have the worst of this ? Dost thou know whom thou disobeyest, and contendest with, and what thou art doing ? It were a far wiser and easier task for thee to contend with the thorns, and spurn them with thy bare feet, and beat them with thy bare hands, or put thine head into the burning fire. " Be not deceived, God will not be mocked." Gal. 6 : 7. Whoever else be mocked, God will not: you had better play with the fire in your thatch, than with the fire of his burning wrath. " For our God is a consuming fire." Heb. 12 : 29. O how unmeet a match art thou for God ! " It is a fearful thing to fall into his hands." Heb. 10 : 31. And therefore it is a fearful thing to contend with him, or resist him. As you love your own souls, take heed what you do: what will you say if he begin in wrath to plead with you ? What will you do if he take you once in hand ? will you then strive against his judgment, as now ye do against his grace ? Isa. 27 : 4, 5. " *Fury is not in me :*" saith the Lord : (that is) I delight not to destroy you : I do it, as it were unwillingly ; but yet " *who will set the briers and thorns against me in battle? I would go through them, I would burn them together. Or let him take hold of my strength, that he may make peace with me.*" It is an unequal combat for the briers and stubble to make war with the fire.

And thus you see who it is that calleth you, that would move you to hear his call, and turn: so consider also by what instruments, and how often, and how earnestly he doth it.

1. Every leaf of the blessed book of God hath, as it were, a voice, and calls out to thee, Turn, and live ; turn, or thou wilt die. How canst thou open it, and read a leaf, or hear a chapter, and not perceive God bids thee turn ?

2. It is the voice of every sermon that thou hearest: for what else is the scope and drift of all, but to call, and persuade, and entreat thee to turn.

3. It is the voice of many a motion of the Spirit that secretly speaks over these words again, and urgeth thee to turn.

4. It is likely, sometimes it is the voice of thy own conscience. Art thou not sometimes convinced that all is not well with thee? And doth not thy conscience tell thee that thou must be a new man, and take a new course, and often call upon thee to return?

5. It is the voice of the gracious examples of the godly. When thou seest them live a heavenly life, and fly from the sin which is thy delight, this really calls on thee to turn.

6. It is the voice of all the works of God: for they also are God's books that teach thee this lesson, by showing thee his greatness, and wisdom, and goodness; and calling thee to observe them, and admire the Creator. Psalm 19 : 1, 2. " The heavens declare the glory of God, and the firmament showeth his handy work : day unto day uttereth speech, night unto night showeth knowledge." Every time the sun riseth unto thee, it really calleth thee to turn, as if it should say, " What do I travel and compass the world for, but to declare to men the glory of their Maker, and to light them to do his work? And do I still find thee doing the work of sin, and sleeping out thy life in negligence? Awake thou that sleepest, and arise from the dead, and Christ shall give thee light." Ephes. 5 : 14. " The night is far spent, the day is at hand; it is now high time to awake out of sleep. Let us therefore cast off the works of darkness, and let us put on the armor of light. Let us walk honestly as in the day, not in rioting and drunkenness, not in chambering and wantonness, not in strife and envying, but put ye on the Lord Jesus Christ, and make not provision for the flesh, to fulfil the lusts thereof." Rom. 13 : 11, 14. This text was the means of Austin's conversion.

7. It is the voice of every mercy thou dost possess; if thou couldst but hear and understand them, they all cry out unto thee, Turn. Why doth the earth bear thee, but to seek and serve the Lord? Why doth it afford thee its fruits, but to serve him? Why doth the air afford thee breath, but to serve him? Why do all the creatures serve thee with their labors and their lives, but that thou mightest serve the Lord of them and thee? Why doth he give thee time, and health, and strength, but only to serve him? Why hast thou meat, and drink, and clothes, but for his service? Hast thou any thing which thou hast not received? and if thou didst receive them, it is reason thou shouldst bethink thee from whom, and to what end and use thou didst receive them. Didst thou never cry to him for help in thy distress, and didst thou not then understand that it was thy part to turn and serve him, if he would deliver thee? He hath done his part, and spared thee yet longer, and tried thee another, and another year; and yet dost thou not turn? You know the parable of the unfruitful fig-tree, Luke, 13 : 7, 9. When the Lord had said, " Cut it down, why cumbereth it the ground?" he was entreated to try it one year longer, and then if it proved not fruitful, to cut it down. Christ himself there makes the application twice over, (ver. 3 and 5.) " Except ye repent, ye shall all likewise perish." How many years hath God looked for the fruits of love and holiness from thee, and hath found none, and yet he hath spared thee? How many a time, by thy wilful ignorance, and carelessness, and disobedience, hast thou provoked justice to say, " Cut him down, why cumbereth he the ground?" And yet mercy hath prevailed, and patience hath forborne the fatal blow, to this day. If thou hadst the understanding of a man within thee, thou wouldst know that all this calleth thee to turn. " Dost thou think thou shalt still escape the judgment of God? or despisest thou the riches of his goodness, and forbearance, and long-suffering? not knowing that the goodness of God leadeth thee to repentance. But, after thy hardness and impenitent heart, treasurest up unto thyself wrath against the day of wrath, and revelation of the righteous judgment of God, who will render to every man according to his deeds." Rom. 2 : 3–6.

8. Moreover, it is the voice of every affliction to call thee to make haste and turn. Sickness and pain cry, Turn : and poverty, and loss of friends, and every twig of the chastening rod, cry, Turn. And yet wilt thou not hearken to the call? These have come near thee, and made thee feel; they have made thee groan, and can they not make thee turn?

9. The very frame of thy nature and being itself, bespeaketh thy return. Why hast thou reason, but to rule thy flesh, and serve thy Lord? Why hast thou an understanding soul, but to learn and know his will and do it? Why hast thou a heart within thee that can love, and fear, and desire, but that thou shouldst fear him, and love him, and desire after him?

Lay all these together now, and see what should be the issue. The holy Scriptures call upon thee to turn; the ministers of Christ call upon thee to turn; the Spirit cries, Turn; thy conscience cries, Turn; the godly, by persuasions and example cry, Turn; the whole world, and all the creatures therein that are presented to thy consideration cry, Turn; the patient forbearance of God cries, Turn; all the mercies which thou receivest cry, Turn; the rod of God's

chastisement cries Turn; thy reason and the frame of
thy nature bespeaks thy turning; and so do all thy
promises to God; and yet art thou not resolved to
turn?

III. Moreover, poor hard-hearted sinner, didst thou
ever consider upon what terms thou standest all this
while with Him that calleth on thee to turn? Thou
art his own, and owest him thyself, and all thou hast;
and may he not command his own? Thou art his
absolute servant, and shouldst serve no other master.
Thou standest at his mercy, and thy life is in his
hand, and he is resolved to save thee upon no other
terms; thou hast many malicious spiritual enemies
that would be glad if God would but forsake thee,
and let them alone with thee, and leave thee to their
will; how quickly would they deal with thee in another manner! and thou canst not be delivered from
them but by turning unto God. Thou art fallen un
der his wrath by thy sin already; and thou knowest
not how long his patience will yet wait. Perhaps this
is the last year, perhaps the last day. His sword is
even at thy heart while the word is in thine ear;
and if thou turn not, thou art a dead and undone
man. Were thy eyes but open to see where thou
standest, even upon the brink of hell, and to see how
many thousands are there already that did not turn,
thou wouldst see that it is time to look about thee.

Well, sirs, look inwards now and tell me how your
hearts are affected with those offers of the Lord. You
hear what is his mind: he delighteth not in your
death; he calls to you, Turn, turn: it is a fearful sign
if all this move thee not, or if it do but half move thee,
and much more if it make thee more careless in thy
misery, because thou hearest of the mercifulness of

God. The working of the medicine will partly tell
us whether there be any hope of the cure. O what
glad tidings would it be to those that are now in hell,
if they had but such a message from God! What a
joyful word would it be to hear this, Turn and live!
Yea, what a welcome word would it be to thyself,
when thou hast felt that wrath of God but an hour!
Or, if after a thousand or ten thousand years' torment,
thou couldst but hear such a word from God, Turn
and live; and yet wilt thou neglect it, and suffer us
to return without our errand?

Behold, sinners, we are sent here as the messengers
of the Lord, to set before you life and death. What
say you? which of them will you choose? Christ
standeth, as it were, by thee, with heaven in the one
hand, and hell in the other, and offereth thee thy
choice. Which wilt thou choose? The voice of the
Lord maketh the rocks to tremble. Psalm 29. And is
it nothing to hear him threaten thee, if thou wilt not
turn? Dost thou not understand and feel this voice,
" Turn ye, turn ye, why will ye die?" Why? It is
the voice of love, of infinite love, of thy best and kindest
friend, as thou mightest easily perceive by the motion;
and yet canst thou neglect it? It is the voice of pity
and compassion. The Lord seeth whither thou art
going better than thou dost, which makes him call
after thee, Turn, turn. He seeth what will become
of thee, if thou turn not. He thinketh with himself,
" Ah! this poor sinner will cast himself into endless
torments if he do not turn. I must in justice deal with
him according to my righteous law." And therefore
he calleth after thee, Turn, turn. O sinner! If thou
didst but know the thousandth part, as well as God
doth, the danger that is near you, and the misery

that you are running into, we should have no more
need to call after you to turn.

Moreover, this voice that calleth to thee is the same
that hath prevailed with thousands already, and called
all to heaven that are now there; and they would not
now for a thousand worlds that they had made light
of it, and not turned to God. Now, what are they
possessing that turned at God's call? Now they perceive that it was indeed the voice of love, that meant
them no more harm than their salvation; and if thou
wilt obey the same call thou shalt come to the same
happiness. There are millions that must for ever lament that they turned not; but there is never a soul
in heaven that is sorry that they were converted.

Well, sirs, are you yet resolved, or are you not?
Do I need to say any more to you? What will you
do? Will you turn or not? Speak, man, in thy heart,
to God, though you speak not out to me; speak, lest
he take thy silence for denial; speak quickly, lest he
never make thee the like offer more; speak resolvedly,
and not waveringly, for he will have no indifferents
to be his followers. Say in thine heart now, without
any more delay, even before thou stir hence, " By the
grace of God I am resolved presently to turn. And
because I know my own insufficiency, I am resolved
to wait on God for his grace, and to follow him in his
ways, and forsake my former courses and companions.
and give up myself to the guidance of the Lord."

Sirs, you are not shut up in the darkness of hea-
thenism, nor in the desperation of the damned. Life
is before you, and you may have it on reasonable
terms, if you will; yea, on free cost, if you will accept
it. The way of God lieth plain before you; the church
is open to you. You may have Christ, and pardon,

and holiness, if you will. What say you? Will you
or will you not? If you say nay, or say nothing, and
still go on, God is witness, and this congregation is
witness, and your own consciences are witnesses, how
fair an offer you had this day. Remember, you might
have had Christ, and would not. Remember, when
you have lost it, that you might have had eternal life,
as well as others, and would not; and all because you
would not turn!

But let us come to the next doctrine, and hear your
reasons.

DOCTRINE VI

*The Lord condescendeth to reason the case with
unconverted sinners, and to ask them why they
will die.*

A strange disputation it is, both as to the controversy and as to the disputants.

I. The controversy, or question propounded to dispute of is, Why wicked men will destroy themselves?
or, Why they will rather die than turn; whether
they have any sufficient reason for so doing?

II. The disputants are God and man: the most
holy God, and wicked unconverted sinners.

Is it not a strange thing, which God doth here seem
to suppose, that any man should be willing to die and
be damned? yea, that this should be the case of the
wicked? that is, of the greatest part of the world. But
you will say, "This cannot be; for nature desireth
the preservation and felicity of itself; and the wicked
are more selfish than others, and not less; and therefore how can any man be willing to be damned?"

To which I answer:—1. It is a certain truth that

no man can be willing to bear any evil, as evil, but only as it hath some appearance of good; much less can any man be willing to be eternally tormented. Misery, as such, is desired by none. 2. But yet for all that, it is most true which God here teacheth us, that the cause why the wicked die is, because they will die. And this is true in several respects.

1. Because they will go the way that leads to hell, although they are told by God and man whither it goes and whither it ends; and though God hath so often professed in his word, that if they hold on in that way they shall be condemned; and that they shall not be saved unless they turn. Isa. 48 : 22; 57 : 21; 59 : 8, " There is no peace, saith the Lord, to the wicked." " The way of peace they know not; there is no judgment in their goings; they have made them crooked paths. Whosoever goeth therein shall not know peace." They have the word and the oath of the living God for it, that if they will not turn they shall not enter into his rest: and yet, wicked they are, and wicked they will be, let God and man say what they will: fleshly they are, and fleshly they will be, worldlings they are, and worldlings they will be, though God hath told them that the love of the world is enmity to God, and that if any man love the world (in that measure) the love of the Father is not in him James, 4 : 4; 1 John, 2 : 15. So that, consequently, these men are willing to be damned, though not directly; they are willing to walk in the way to hell, and love the certain cause of their torment; though they do not will hell itself, and do not love the pain which they must endure.

Is not this the truth of your case sirs ? You would not burn in hell, but you will kindle the fire by your sins, and cast yourselves into it; you would not be tormented with devils for ever, but you will do that which will certainly procure it in spite of all that can be said against it. It is just as if you would say, " I will drink this poison, but yet I will not die. I will cast myself headlong from the top of a steeple, but yet I will not kill myself. I will thrust this knife into my heart, but yet I will not take away my life. I will put this fire into the thatch of my house, but yet I will not burn it." Just so it is with wicked men; they will be wicked, and they will live after the flesh and the world, and yet they would not be damned. But do you not know that the means lead to the end? and that God hath, by his righteous law, concluded that ye must repent or perish? He that will take poison may as well say plainly, I will kill myself, for it will prove no better in the end; though perhaps he loved it for the sweetness of the sugar that was mixed with it, and would not be persuaded that it was poison, but that he might take it and do well enough; but it is not his conceits and confidence that will save his life. So if you will be drunkards, or fornicators, or worldlings, or live after the flesh, you may as well say plainly, We will be damned; for so you will be unless you turn. Would you not rebuke the folly of a murderer that would say I will kill, but I will not be hanged, when he knows that if he does the one, the judge in justice will see that the other be done? If he say I will murder, he may as well say plainly, I will be hanged; and if you will go on in a carnal life, you may as well say plainly, We will go to hell.

2. Moreover, the wicked will not use those means without which there is no hope of their salvation. He that will not eat, may as well say plainly, he will

not live, unless he can tell how to live without meat.
He that will not go his journey, may as well say
plainly he will not come to the end. He that falls into
the water, and will not come out, nor suffer another
to help him out, may as well say plainly, he will be
drowned. So if you be carnal and ungodly, and will
not be converted, nor use the means by which you
should be converted, but think it more ado than needs,
you may as well say plainly you will be damned; for
if you have found out a way to be saved without conversion, you have done that which was never done
before.

3. Yea, this is not all; but the wicked are unwilling
even to partake of salvation itself; though they may
desire somewhat which they call by the name of heaven, yet heaven itself, considered in the true nature
of the felicity, they desire not; yea, their hearts are
quite against it. Heaven is a state of perfect holiness,
and of continual love and praise to God, and the
wicked have no heart to this. The imperfect love,
and praise, and holiness, which is here to be attained,
they have no mind for; much less for that which is
so much greater. The joys of heaven are of so pure
and spiritual a nature that the heart of the wicked
cannot truly desire them.

So that by this time you may see on what ground
it is that God supposeth that the wicked are willing
their own destruction. They will not turn, though
they must turn or die: they will rather venture on
certain misery than be converted; and then to quiet
themselves in their sins, they will make themselves
believe that they shall nevertheless escape.

II. And as this controversy is matter of wonder, in
that men should be such enemies to themselves as

wilfully to cast away their souls, so are the disputants too : that God should stoop so low as thus to plead the case with men; and that men should be so strangely blind and obstinate as to need all this in so plain a case; yea, and to resist all this, when their own salvation lieth upon the issue.

No wonder that they will not hear us that are men when they will not hear the Lord himself. As God saith, (Ezek. 3 : 7,) when he sent the prophet to the Israelites, " The house of Israel will not hearken unto thee; for they will not hearken unto me; for all the house of Israel are impudent and hard-hearted." No wonder if they can plead against a minister, or a godly neighbor, when they will plead against the Lord himself, even against the plainest passages of his word, and think that they have reason on their side. When they weary the Lord with their words, they say, " Wherein have we wearied him?" Mal. 2 : 17. The priests that despised his name durst ask, " Wherein have we despised thy name?" And " when they polluted his altar, and made the table of the Lord contemptible," they durst say, " Wherein have we polluted thee?" Mal. 1 : 6, 7. But " Wo unto him (saith the Lord) that striveth with his Maker! Let the potsherds strive with the potsherds of the earth : shall the clay say to him that fashioneth it, What makest thou ?"

Quest. But why is it that God will reason the case with man ?

Answ. 1. Because that man being a reasonable creature, is accordingly to be dealt with, and by reason to be persuaded and overcome; God hath therefore endowed them with reason, that they might use it for him. One would think a reasonable creature should not go against the clearest, the greatest reason in the world, when it is set before him.

2. At least, men shall see that God did require nothing of them that was unreasonable; but both in what he commandeth them, and what he forbids them, he hath all the right reason in the world on his side; and they have good reason to obey him—but none to disobey him. And thus even the damned shall be forced to justify God, and confess that it was only reasonable that they should have turned to him; and they shall be forced to condemn themselves, and confess that they had little reason to cast away themselves by the neglecting of his grace in the day of their visitation.

USE.—Look up your best and strongest reasons, sinners, if you will make good your way. You see now with whom you have to deal. What sayest thou, unconverted sensual sinner? Darest thou venture upon a dispute with God? Art thou able to confute him? Art thou ready to enter the lists? God asketh thee, Why wilt thou die? Art thou furnished with a sufficient answer? Wilt thou undertake to prove that God is mistaken, and that thou art in the right? O what an undertaking is that! Why, either he or you are mistaken, when he is for your conversion, and you are against it: he calls upon you to turn, and you will not; he bids you do it presently, even to-day, while it is called to-day, and you delay, and think it time enough hereafter. He saith it must be a total change, and you must be holy and new creatures, and born again: and you think that less may serve the turn, and that it is enough to patch up the old man, without becoming new. Who is in the right now?

God or you? God calleth you to turn, and to live a
holy life, and you will not; by your disobedient lives
it appears you will not. If you will, why do you not?
Why have you not done it all this while? And why
do you not fall upon it yet? Your wills have the
command of your lives. We may certainly conclude
that you are unwilling to turn when you do not turn.
And why will you not?

Can you give any reason for it that is worthy to
be called a reason?

I that am but a worm, your fellow creature, of a
shallow capacity, dare challenge the wisest of you
all to reason the case with me while I plead my Maker's cause; and I need not be discouraged when I
know I plead but the cause that God pleadeth, and
contend for him that will have the best at last. Had
I but these two general grounds against you, I am
sure that you have no good reason on your side.

I am sure it can be no good reason which is against
the God of truth and reason. It cannot be light that
is contrary to the sun. There is no knowledge in any
creature but what it had from God; and therefore
none can be wiser than God. It were fatal presumption for the highest angel to compare with his Creator! What is it then for a lump of earth, an ignorant
sot, that knoweth not himself nor his own soul, that
knoweth but little of the things which he seeth, yea,
that is more ignorant than many of his neighbors, to
set himself against the wisdom of the Lord! It is one
of the fullest discoveries of the horrible wickedness of
carnal men, and the stark madness of such as sin,
that so silly a mole dare contradict his Maker, and
call in question the word of God: yea, that those
people in our parishes that are so ignorant that they

cannot give us a reasonable answer concerning the
very principles of religion, are yet so wise in their
own conceit, that they dare question the plainest
truths of God, yea, contradict them, and cavil against
them, when they can scarcely speak sense, and will
believe them no further than agreeth with their foolish wisdom!

And as I know that God must needs be in the right,
so I know the cause is so palpable and gross which
he pleadeth against, that no man can have reason
for it. Is it possible that a man can have any reason
to break his Maker's laws, and reason to dishonor the
Lord of glory, and reason to abuse the Lord that
bought him? Is it possible that a man can have any
good reason to damn his own immortal soul? Mark the
Lord's question, Turn ye, turn ye, why will ye die?
Is eternal death a thing to be desired? Are you in love
with hell? What reason have you wilfully to perish?
If you think you have some reason to sin, should you
not remember that death is the wages of sin, (Rom.
6: 23.) and think whether you have any reason to
undo yourselves, body and soul for ever? You should
not only ask whether you love the adder, but whether
you love the sting? It is such a thing for a man to cast
away his everlasting happiness, and to sin against
God, that no good reason can be given for it; but the
more any one pleads for it, the more mad he showeth
himself to be. Had you a lordship, or a kingdom
offered you for every sin that you commit, it were not
reason, but madness to accept it. Could you by every
sin obtain the highest thing on earth that flesh desireth,
it were of no considerable value to persuade you in
reason to commit it. If it were to please your greatest or dearest friends, or to obey the greatest prince on

earth, or to save your lives, or to escape the greatest
earthly misery; all these are of no consideration to
draw a man in reason to the committing of one sin.
If it were a right hand, or a right eye that would
hinder your salvation, it is the most gainful way to
cast it away, rather than to go to hell to save it; for
there is no saving a part when you lose the whole.
So exceedingly great are the matters of eternity, that
nothing in this world deserveth once to be named in
comparison with them; nor can any earthly thing,
though it were life, or crowns, or kingdoms, be a reasonable excuse for the neglect of matters of such high
and everlasting consequence. A man can have no
reason to cross his ultimate end. Heaven is such a
thing, that if you lose it, nothing can supply the want,
or make up the loss; and hell is such a thing, that if
you suffer it, nothing can remove your misery, or give
you ease and comfort; and therefore nothing can
be a valuable consideration to excuse you for neglecting your own salvation; for, saith our Savior,
" What shall it profit a man if he shall gain the
whole world, and lose his own soul?" Mark, 8 : 36.

O sirs, that you did but know what matters they are
that we are now speaking to you of! you would have
other kind of thoughts of these things. If the devil
could come to the saints in heaven that live in the
sight and love of God, and should offer them sensual
pleasures, or merry company, or sports to entice them
away from God and glory, I pray you tell me, how do
you think they would entertain the motion? Nay, or
if he should offer them to be kings on the earth, do you
think this would entice them down from heaven? O
with what hatred and holy scorn would they reject
the motion! And why should not you do so, that have

heaven opened to your faith, if you had but faith to see it? There is never a soul in hell but knows, by this time, that it was a mad exchange to let go heaven for fleshly pleasure: and that it is not a little mirth, or pleasure, or worldly riches, or honor, or the good will or word of men, that will quench hell fire, or make him a gainer that loseth his soul. O if you had heard what I believe, if you had seen what I believe, and that on the credit of the word of God, you would say there can be no reason to warrant a man to destroy his soul; you durst not sleep quietly another night, before you had resolved to turn and live. *

If you see a man put his hand in the fire till it burn off, you will marvel at it; but this is a thing that a man may have a reason for, as Bishop Cranmer had when he burnt off his hand for subscribing to Popery. If you see a man cut off a leg, or an arm, it is a sad sight; but this is a thing that a man may have a good reason for, as many a man hath it done to save his life. If you see a man give his body to be tormented with scourges and racks, or to be burned to ashes, and refuse deliverance when it is offered, this is a hard case to flesh and blood; but this a man may have good reason for, as you may see in Heb. 11 : 33, 36, and as many a hundred martyrs have done. But for a man to forsake the Lord that made him, and to run into the fire of hell when he is told of it, and entreated to turn that he may be saved—this is a thing that can have no reason in the world to justify or excuse it. For heaven will pay for the loss of any thing that we can lose to obtain it, or for any labor which we bestow for it; but nothing can pay for the loss of heaven.

I beseech you now let this word come nearer to your

heart. As you are convinced that you have no reason to destroy yourselves, so tell me what reason have you to refuse to turn and live to God? What reason has the veriest worldling, or drunkard, or ignorant careless sinner of you all, why he should not be as holy as any you know, and be as careful for his soul as any other? Will not hell be as intolerable to you as to others? Should not your own souls be as dear to you as theirs to them? Hath not God as much authority over you? Why then will you not become a sanctified people, as well as they?

O, sirs, when God bringeth the matter down to the very principles of nature, and shows that you have no more reason to be ungodly than you have to damn your own souls—if yet you will not understand and turn, it seems a desperate case that you are in.

And now, either you have good reason for what you do, or you have not: if not, will you go against reason itself? Will you do that which you have no reason for? But if you think you have a reason, produce it, and make the best of your matter. Reason the case a little with me, your fellow creature, which is far easier than to reason the case with God; tell me, man, here before the Lord, as if thou wert to die this hour, why shouldest thou not resolve to turn this day, before thou stir from the place thou standest in; what reason hast thou to deny or to delay? Hast thou any reasons that satisfy thine own conscience for it, or any that thou darest own and plead at the bar of God? If thou hast, let us hear them, bring them forth, and make them good. But, alas! what poor stuff, what nonsense, instead of reasons, do we daily hear from ungodly men! But for their necessity I should be ashamed to name them.

Objection 1. One saith, if none shall be saved but such converted and sanctified ones as you talk of, then heaven would be but empty; then God help a great many!

Answer. Why, it seems you think that God doth not know, or else that he is not to be believed! Measure not all by yourselves: God hath thousands and millions of his sanctified ones; but yet they are few in comparison of the world, as Christ himself hath told us, Matt. 7 : 13, 14. Luke, 11 : 32. It better beseems you to make that use of this truth which Christ teacheth you: " Strive to enter in at the strait gate ; for strait is the gate and narrow is the way that leadeth unto life, and few there be that find it; but wide is the gate and broad is the way which leadeth to destruction, and many there be that go in thereat." Luke, 13 : 22—24. Fear not, little flock, (saith Christ to his sanctified ones,) for it is your Father's good pleasure to give you the kingdom. Luke, 12 : 32.

Object. 2. I am sure, if such as I go to hell, we shall have store of company.

Answ. And will that be any ease or comfort to you? Or do you think you may not have company enough in heaven? Will you be undone for company, or will you not believe that God will execute his threatenings, because there be so many that are guilty? These are all unreasonable conceits.

Object. 3. But all men are sinners, even the best of you all.

Answ. But all are not unconverted sinners. The godly live not in gross sins ; and their very infirmities are their grief and burden, which they daily long, and pray, and strive to be rid of. Sin hath not dominion over them.

Object. 4. I do not see that professors are any better than other men; they will overreach, and oppress, and are as covetous as any.

Answ. Whatever hypocrites are, it is not so with those that are sanctified. God hath thousands, and tens of thousands that are otherwise, though the malicious world doth accuse them of what they can never prove, and of that which never entered into their hearts; and commonly they charge them with heart-sins, which none can see but God, because they can charge them with no such wickedness in their lives as they are guilty of themselves.

Object. 5. But I am no whoremonger, nor drunkard, nor oppressor; and therefore why should you call upon me to be converted?

Answ. As if you were not born after the flesh, and had not lived after the flesh, as well as others! Is it not as great a sin as any of these, for a man to have an earthly mind, and to love the world above God, and to have an unbelieving, unhumbled heart? Nay, let me tell you more, that many persons that avoid disgraceful sins are as fast glued to the world, and as much slaves to the flesh, and as strange to God, and averse to heaven in their more civil course, as others are in their more shameful notorious sins.

Object. 6. But I mean nobody any harm, nor do any harm; and why then should God condemn me?

Answ. Is it no harm to neglect the Lord that made thee, and the work for which thou camest into the world, and to prefer the creature before the Creator, and to neglect grace that is daily offered thee? It is the depth of thy sinfulness to be so insensible of it: the dead feel not that they are dead. If once thou wert made alive, thou wouldst see more amiss in thy self, and marvel at thyself for making so light of it.

Object. 7. I think you would make men mad, under pretence of converting them: it is enough to rack the brains of simple people to muse so much on matters so high for them.

Answ. 1. Can you be more mad than you are already? or, at least, can there be a more dangerous madness than to neglect your everlasting welfare, and wilfully undo yourselves?

2. A man is never well in his wits till he be converted: he never knows God, nor knows sin, nor knows Christ, nor knows the world, nor himself, nor what his business is on earth, so as to set himself about it, till he be converted. The Scripture saith, that the wicked are unreasonable men, (2 Thess. 3 : 2,) and that the wisdom of the world is foolishness with God. 1 Cor. 1 : 20. and Luke 15 : 17. It is said of the prodigal, that when he came to himself he resolved to return. What a strange wisdom is this; men will disobey God, and run to hell, for fear of being out of their wits?

3. What is there in the work that Christ calls you to, that should drive a man out of his wits? Is it the loving God, and calling upon him, and comfortably thinking of the glory to come, and the forsaking of our sins, and loving one another, and delighting ourselves in the service of God? Are these such things as should make men mad?

4. And whereas you say that these matters are too high for us; you accuse God himself for making this our work, and giving us his word, and commanding all that will be blessed to meditate on it day and night. Are the matters which we are made for, and which we live for, too high for us to meddle with? This is

plainly to unman us, and to make beasts of us, as if we were like them that must meddle with no higher matters than what belongs to flesh and earth. If heaven be too high for you to think on and provide for, it will be too high for you ever to possess.

5. If God should sometimes suffer any weak-headed persons to be distracted by thinking of eternal things, this is because they misunderstand them, and run without a guide; and of the two, I had rather be in the case of such a one, than of the mad unconverted world, that take their distraction to be their wisdom.

Object. 8. I do not think that God cares so much what men think, or speak, or do, as to make so great a matter of it.

Answ. It seems, then, you take the word of God to be false: then what will you believe? But your own reason might teach you better, if you believe not the scriptures; for you see God sets not so light by us but that he vouchsafed to make us, and still preserveth us, and daily upholdeth us, and provideth for us; and will any wise man make a curious frame for nothing? Will you make or buy a clock or watch, and daily look at it, and not care whether it go true or false? Surely, if you believe not a particular eye of Providence observing your hearts and lives, you cannot believe or expect any particular Providence to observe your wants and troubles, or to relieve you; and if God had so little care for you as you imagine, you would never have lived till now; a hundred diseases would have striven which should first destroy you; yea, the devils would have haunted you, and fetched you away alive, as the great fishes devour the less, and as ravenous beasts and birds devour others. You cannot think that God made man for no end or use;

and if he made him for any, it was surely for himself; and can you think he cares not whether his end be accomplished, and whether we do the work that we are made for?

Yea, by this atheistical objection you make God to have made and upheld all the world in vain; for what are all other lower creatures for, but for man? What doth the earth but bear us and nourish us, and the beasts but serve us with their labors and lives, and so of the rest? And hath God made so glorious a habitation, and set man to dwell in it, and made all his servants; and now doth he look for nothing at his hands, nor care how he thinks, or speaks, or lives? This is most unreasonable.

Object. 9. It was a better world when men did not make so much ado in religion.

Answ. 1. It hath ever been the custom to praise the times past; that world that you speak of was wont to say it was a better world in their forefathers' days; and so did they of their forefathers. This is but an old custom, because we all feel the evil of our own times, but we see not that which was before us.

2. Perhaps you speak as you think. Worldlings think the world is at the best when it is agreeable to their minds, and when they have most mirth and worldly pleasure; and I doubt not but the devil, as well as you, would say, that then it was a better world, for then he had more service, and less disturbance. But the world is at the best when God is most loved, regarded, and obeyed; and how else will you know when the world is good or bad, but by this?

Object. 10. There are so many ways and religions, that we know not which to be of, and therefore we will be even as we are.

Answ. Because there are many, will you be of that way that you may be sure is wrong? None are further out of the way than worldly, fleshly, unconverted sinners; for they do not only err in this or that opinion, as many sects do, but in the very scope and drift of their lives. If you were going a journey that your life lay on, would you stop, or turn again, because you met with some cross-ways, or because you saw some travellers go the horse-way, and some the foot-way, and some perhaps break over the hedge, yea, and some miss the way? Or would you not rather be the more careful to inquire the way? If you have some servants that know not how to do your work right, and some that are unfaithful, would you take it well of any of the rest that would therefore be idle and do you no service, because they see their companions so bad?

Object. 11. I do not see that it goes any better with those that are so godly, than with other men; they are as poor and in as much trouble as others.

Answ. And perhaps in much more, when God sees it meet. They take not earthly prosperity for their wages; they have laid up their treasure and hopes in another world, or else they are not Christians indeed; the less they have, the more is behind, and they are content to wait till then.

Object. 12. When you have said all that you can, I am resolved to hope well, and trust in God, and do as well as I can, and not make so much ado.

Answ. 1. Is that doing as well as you can, when you will not turn to God, but your heart is against his holy and diligent service? It is as well as you will, indeed, but that is your misery.

2. My desire is, that you should hope and trust in

God. But for what is it that you will hope? Is it to
be saved, if you turn and be sanctified? For this you
have God's promise, and therefore hope for it, and
spare not. But if you hope to be saved without conversion, and a holy life, this is not to hope in God, but
in Satan, or yourselves; for God hath given you no
such promise, but told you the contrary; but it is
Satan and self-love that made you such promises, and
raised you to such hopes.

Well, if these, and such as these, be all you have
to say against conversion, and a holy life, your all is
nothing, and worse than nothing; and if these, and
such as these, seem reasons sufficient to persuade you
to forsake God, and cast yourselves into hell, the Lord
deliver you from such reasons, and from such blind
understandings, and from such senseless hardened
hearts. Dare you stand to aver one of these reasons
at the bar of God? Do you think it will then serve
your turn to say, " Lord, I did not turn, because I had
so much to do in the world, or because I did not like
the lives of some professors, or because I saw men of
so many minds!" O how easily will the light of that
day confound and shame such reasonings as these!
Had you the world to look after? Let the world which
you served now pay you your wages, and save you if
it can. Had you not a better world to look after first,
and were ye not commanded to seek first God's kingdom and righteousness, and promised that other things
should be added to you? Matt. 6 : 33. And were ye
not told, that godliness was profitable to all things,
having the promise of this life, and that which is to
come? 1 Tim. 4 : 8. Did the sins of the professors
hinder you? You should rather have been the more
heedful, and learned by their falls to beware, and have

been the more careful, and not to be more careless. It was the Scripture, and not their lives, that was your rule. Did the many opinions of the world hinder you? Why the Scripture that was your rule did teach you but one way, and that was the right way. If you had followed that, even in so much as was plain and easy, you should never have miscarried. Will not such answers as these confound and silence you? If these will not, God hath those that will. When he asked the man, "Friend, how camest thou in hither, not having on a wedding garment?" Matt. 22 : 12, that is, what dost thou in my church among professed Christians, without a holy heart and life—what answer did he make? Why, the text saith, "he was speechless;" he had nothing to say. The clearness of the case, and the majesty of God, will then easily stop the mouths of the most confident of you, though you will not be put down by any thing we can say to you now, but will make good your cause be it ever so bad. I know already that never a reason that now you can give me will do you any good at last, when your case must be opened before the Lord, and all the world.

Nay, I scarce think that your own consciences are well satisfied with your reasons; for if they are, it seems, then, you have not so much as a purpose to repent. But if you do purpose to repent, it seems you do not put much confidence in your reasons which you bring against it.

What say you, unconverted sinners? Have you any good reasons to give why you should not turn, and presently turn with all your hearts? Or will you go to hell in despite of reason itself? Bethink you what you do in time, for it will shortly be too late to

bethink you. Can you find any fault with God, or
his work, or his wages? Is he a bad master? Is the
devil, whom ye serve, a better? or is the flesh a better? Is there any harm in a holy life? Is a life of
worldliness and ungodliness better? Do you think in
your consciences that it would do you any harm to be
converted and live a holy life? What harm can it
do you? Is it harm to you to have the Spirit of Christ
within you, and to have a cleansed purified heart?
If it be bad to be holy, why doth God say, " Be ye
holy, for I am holy?" 1 Pet. 1 : 15, 16; Lev. 20 : 7.
Is it evil to be like God? Is it not said that God made
man in his own image? Why, this holiness is his
image; this Adam lost, and this Christ by his word
and Spirit would restore to you, as he doth to all that
he will save. Tell me truly, as before the Lord,
though you are loth to live a holy life, had you not
rather die in the case of those that do so, than of
others? If you were to die this day, had you not rather die in the case of a converted man than of an unconverted? of a holy and heavenly man than of a
carnal earthly man? and would you not say as Ba-
laam, (Numb. 23 : 10.) " Let me die the death of the
righteous, and let my last end be like his!" And why
will you not now be of the mind that you will be of
then? First or last you must come to this, either to
be converted, or to wish you had been, when it is
too late.

But what is it that you are afraid of losing, if you
turn? Is it your friends? You will but change them;
God will be your friend, and Christ and the Spirit
will be your friend; and every Christian will be your
friend. You will get one friend that will stand you in
more stead than all the friends in the world could have

done. The friends you lose would have but enticed
you to hell, but could not have delivered you : but the
friend you get will save you from hell, and bring you
to his own eternal rest.

Is it your pleasures that you are afraid of losing?
You think you shall never have a merry day again
if once you be converted. Alas! that you should think
it a greater pleasure to live in foolish sports and mer-
riments, and please your flesh, than to live in the believing thoughts of glory, and in the love of God, and
in righteousness, and peace, and joy in the Holy
Ghost, in which the state of grace consisteth. Rom.
14 : 17. If it would be a greater pleasure for you to
think of your lands and inheritance, if you were lord
of all the country, than it is for a child to play at pins,
why should it not be a greater joy to you to think of
the kingdom of heaven being yours, than of all the
riches or pleasures of the world? As it is but foolish
childishness that makes children so delight in toys
that they would not leave them for all your lands, so
it is but foolish worldliness, and fleshliness, and wickedness, that makes you so much delight in your houses
and lands, and meat and drink, and ease and honor,
as that you would not part with them for the heavenly delights. But what will you do for pleasure when
these are gone? Do you not think of that? When
your pleasures end in horror, and go out like a taper,
the pleasures of the saints are then at the best. I have
had myself but a little taste of the heavenly pleasures
in the forethoughts of the blessed approaching day,
and in the present persuasions of the love of God in
Christ; but I have taken too deep a draught of earthly pleasures: so that you may see, if I be partial, it is
on your side; and yet I must profess from that little

experience, that there is no comparison. There is more joy to be had in a day, if the sun of life shine clear upon us, in the state of holiness, than in a whole life of sinful pleasures. "I had rather be a door-keeper in the house of God than to dwell in the tents of wickedness." Psalm 84 : 10. "A day in his courts is better than a thousand" any where else. Psalm 84 : 10. The mirth of the wicked is like the laughter of a madman, that knows not his own misery; and therefore Solomon says of such laughter, "it is mad; and of mirth, what doth it?" Eccles. 2 : 2; 7 : 2, 6. "It is better to go to the house of mourning than to go to the house of feasting; for that is the end of all men, and the living will lay it to his heart. Sorrow is better than laughter; for by the sadness of the countenance the heart is made better. The heart of the wise is in the house of mourning; but the heart of fools is in the house of mirth. It is better to bear the rebuke of the wise, than to hear the song of fools; for as the crackling of thorns under a pot, so is the laughter of the fool." Your loudest laughter is but like that of a man that is tickled; he laughs when he has no cause of joy. Judge, as you are men, whether this be a wise man's part. It is but your carnal unsanctified nature that makes a holy life seem grievous to you, and a course of sensuality seem more delightful. If you will but turn, the Holy Ghost will give you another nature and inclination, and then it will be more pleasant to you to be rid of your sin, than now it is to keep it and you will then say, that you knew not what a comfortable life was till now, and that it was never well with you till God and holiness were your delight.

Question. But how cometh it to pass that men should be so unreasonable in the matters of salvation?

They have wit enough in other matters: what makes them so loth to be converted that there should need so many words in so plain a case, and all will not do, but the most will live and die unconverted?

Answer. To name them only in a few words, the causes are these:

1. Men are naturally in love with the earth and flesh; they are born sinners, and their nature hath an enmity to God and goodness, as the nature of a serpent hath to a man: and when all that we can say goes against an habitual inclination of their natures, no marvel if it prevail little.

2. They are in darkness, and know not the very things they hear. Like a man that was born blind, and hears a high commendation of the light; but what will hearing do, unless he sees it? They know not what God is, nor what is the power of the cross of Christ, nor what the Spirit of holiness is, nor what it is to live in love by faith: they know not the certainty, and suitableness, and excellency of the heavenly inheritance. They know not what conversion and a holy mind and conversation is, even when they hear of it. They are in a mist of ignorance. They are lost and bewildered in sin; like a man that has lost himself in the night, and knows not where he is, nor how to come to himself again, till the daylight recover him.

3. They are wilfully confident that they need no conversion, but some partial amendment, and that they are in the way to heaven already, and are converted when they are not. And if you meet a man that is quite out of his way, you may long enough call on him to turn back again, if he will not believe you that he is out of the way.

4. They are become slaves to their flesh, and drowned in the world, to make provision for it. Their lusts, and passions, and appetites, have distracted them, and got such a hand over them that they cannot tell how to deny them, or how to mind any thing else; so that the drunkard saith, I love a cup of good drink, and I cannot forbear it; the glutton saith, I love good cheer, and I cannot forbear; the fornicator saith, I love to have my lust fulfilled, and I cannot forbear; and the gamester loves to have his sports, and he cannot forbear. So that they are become even captivated slaves to their flesh, and their very wilfulness is become an impotency; and what they would not do, they say they cannot. And the worldling is so taken up with earthly things, that he hath neither heart, nor mind, nor time, for heavenly; but, as in Pharaoh's dream, Gen. 41 : 4, the lean kine did eat up the fat ones; so this lean and barren earth doth eat up all the thoughts of heaven.

5. Some are so carried away by the stream of evil company, that they are possessed with hard thoughts of a godly life, by hearing them speak against it; or at least they think they may venture to do as they see most do, and so they hold on in their sinful ways; and when one is cut off, and cast into hell, and another snatched away from among them to the same condemnation, it doth not much daunt them, because they see not whither they are gone. Poor wretches, they hold on in their ungodliness for all this; for they little know that their companions are now lamenting it in torments. In Luke 16, the rich man in hell would fain have had one to warn his five brethren, lest they should come to that place of torment. It is likely he knew their minds and lives, and knew that they were hasting thither, and little dreamt that he was there, yea, and would little have believed one that should have told them so. I remember a passage that a gentleman, yet living, told me he saw upon a bridge over the Severn.* A man was driving a flock of fat lambs, and something meeting them, and hindering their passage, one of the lambs leapt upon the wall of the bridge, and his legs slipping from under him he fell into the stream; the rest seeing him, did, one after one, leap over the bridge into the stream, and were all or almost all drowned. Those that were behind did little know what was become of them that were gone before; but thought they might venture to follow their companions; but as soon as ever they were over the wall, and falling headlong, the case was altered. Even so it is with unconverted carnal men. One dieth by them, and drops into hell, and another follows the same way; and yet they will go after them, because they think not whither they are gone. O, but when death hath once opened their eyes, and they see what is on the other side of the wall, even in another world, then what would they give to be where they were!

6. Moreover, they have a subtle malicious enemy that is unseen of them, and plays his game in the dark; and it is his principal business to hinder their conversion; and therefore to keep them where they are, by persuading them not to believe the Scriptures, or not to trouble their minds with these matters; or by persuading them to think ill of a godly life, or to think that more is enjoined than need be, and that they may be saved without conversion, and without all this stir; and that God is so merciful that he will not damn any such as they; or at least, that they may

* Mr R. Rowly, of Shrewsbury, upon Acham-Bridge.

stay a little longer, and take their pleasure, and follow the world a little longer yet, and then let it go, and repent hereafter. And by such juggling, deluding cheats as these, the devil keeps the most in his captivity, and leadeth them to his misery.

These, and such like impediments as these, do keep so many thousands unconverted, when God hath done so much, and Christ hath suffered so much, and ministers have said so much for their conversion : when their reasons are silenced and they are not able to answer the Lord that calls after them, " Turn ye, turn ye, why will ye die ?" yet all comes to nothing with the greatest part of them ; and they leave us no more to do after all, but to sit down and lament their wilful misery.

I have now showed you the reasonableness of God's commands, and the unreasonableness of wicked men's disobedience. If nothing will serve their turn, but men will yet refuse to turn, we are next to consider, who is in fault if they be damned. And this brings me to the last doctrine ; which is,

DOCTRINE VII

That if after all this men will not turn, it is not the fault of God that they are condemned, but their own, even their own wilfulness. They die because they will, that is, because they will not turn.

If you will go to hell, what remedy ? God here acquits himself of your blood ; it shall not lie on him if you be lost. A negligent minister may draw it upon him ; and those that encourage you or hinder you not in sin, may draw it upon them ; but be sure of it, it shall not lie upon God. Saith the Lord, concern-

ing his unprofitable vineyard: (Isa. 5 : 1, 4,) "Judge,
I pray you, betwixt me and my vineyard: what
could have been done more to my vineyard that I
have not done in it?" When he had planted it in a
fruitful soil, and fenced it, and gathered out the stones,
and planted it with the choicest vines, what should he
have done more to it? He hath made you men, and
endowed you with reason; he hath furnished you with
all external necessaries; all creatures are at your service; he hath given you a righteous perfect law.
When ye had broken it, and undone yourselves, he
had pity on you, and sent his Son by a miracle of
condescending mercy to die for you, and be a sacrifice
for your sins; and he was in Christ reconciling the
world to himself!

The Lord Jesus hath made you a deed of gift of
himself, and eternal life with him, on the condition
you will but accept it, and return. He hath on this
reasonable condition offered you the free pardon of all
your sins ! he hath written this in his word, and sealed
it by his Spirit, and sent it by his ministers: they
have made the offer to you a hundred and a hundred
times, and called you to accept it, and to turn to God.
They have in his name entreated you, and reasoned
the case with you, and answered all your frivolous
objections. He hath long waited on you, and staid
your leisure, and suffered you to abuse him to his
face ! He hath mercifully sustained you in the midst
of your sins; he hath compassed you about with all
sorts of mercies; he hath also intermixed afflictions,
to remind you of your folly, and call you to your
senses, and his Spirit has been often striving with
your hearts, and saying there, " Turn, sinner, turn
to him that calleth thee. Whither art thou going?

What art thou doing? Dost thou know what will be the end? How long wilt thou hate thy friends, and love thine enemies? When wilt thou let go all, and turn and deliver thyself to God, and give thy Redeemer the possession of thy soul? When shall it once be?" These pleadings have been used with thee, and when thou hast delayed, thou hast been urged to make haste, and God hath called to thee, " To-day, while it is called to-day, harden not thy heart." Why not now without any more delay? Life hath been set before you; the joys of heaven have been opened to you in the Gospel; the certainty of them hath been manifested; the certainty of the everlasting torments of the damned hath been declared to you; unless you would have had a sight of heaven and hell, what could you desire more? Christ hath been, as it were, set forth crucified before your eyes. Gal. 3 : 1. You have been a hundred times told that you are but lost men till you come unto him ; as oft you have been told of the evil of sin, of the vanity of sin, the world, and all the pleasures and wealth it can afford; of the shortness and uncertainty of your lives, and the endless duration of the joy or torment of the life to come. All this, and more than this have you been told, and told again, even till you were weary of hearing it, and till you could make the lighter of it, because you had so often heard it, like the smith's dog, that is brought by custom to sleep under the noise of the hammers and when the sparks fly about his ears ; and though all this have not converted you, yet you are alive, and might have mercy to this day, if you had but hearts to entertain it. And now let reason itself be the judge, whether it be the fault of God or yours, if after this you will be unconverted and be damned. If you die now, it is because you will die. What should be said more to you, or what course should be taken that is more likely to prevail? Are you able to say, and make it good, " We would fain have been converted and become new creatures, but we could not; we would fain have forsaken our sins, but we could not; we would have changed our company, and our thoughts, and our discourse, but we could not." Why could you not, if you would? What hindered you but the wickedness of your hearts? Who forced you to sin, or who held you back from duty? Had not you the same teaching, and time, and liberty to be godly, as your godly neighbors had? Why then could not you have been godly as well as they? Were the church doors shut against you, or did you not keep away yourselves, or sit and sleep, or hear as if you did not hear? Did God put in any exceptions against you in his word, when he invited sinners to return; and when he promised mercy to those that do return? Did he say, " *I* will pardon all that repent except thee?" Did he shut thee out from the liberty of his holy worship? Did he forbid you to pray to him any more than others? You know he did not. God did not drive you away from him, but you forsook him, and ran away yourselves, and when he called you to him, you would not come. If God had excepted you out of the general promise and offer of mercy, or had said to you, " Stand off, I will have nothing to do with such as you; pray not to me, for I will not hear you; if you repent never so much, and cry for mercy never so much, I will not regard you." If God had left you nothing to trust to but desperation, then you had had a fair excuse; you might have said, " To what end do I repent and turn, when

it will do no good?" But this was not your case: you
might have had Christ to be your Lord and Savior,
your head and husband, as well as others, and you
would not, because you felt yourselves not sick enough
for the physician: and because you could not spare
your disease. In your hearts you said as those rebels,
Luke, 19 : 14, "We will not have this man to reign
over us." Christ would have gathered you under
the wings of his salvation, and you would not. Matt.
23 : 37. What desires of your welfare did the Lord
express in his holy word? With what compassion
did he stand over you, and say, "O that my people
had hearkened unto me, and that they had walked in
my ways!" Psalm 17 : 13; 76 : 13, "O that there
were such a heart in this people, that they would fear
me, and keep all my commandments always, that it
might be well with them and with their children for
ever!" Deut. 5 : 29, "O that they were wise, that
they understood this, that they would consider their
latter end!" Deut. 32 : 29. He would have been your
God, and done all for you that your souls could well
desire: but you loved the world and your flesh above
him, and therefore you would not hearken to him:
though you complimented him, and gave him high
titles; yet when it came to the closing, you would
have none of him. Psalm 81 : 11, 12. No marvel then
if he gave you up to your own hearts' lusts, and you
walked in your own counsels. He condescends to reason, and pleads the case with you, and asks you,
"What is there in me, or my service, that you should
be so much against me? What harm have I done
thee, sinner? Have I deserved this unkind dealing at
thy hand? Many mercies have I showed thee: for
which of them dost thou thus despise me? Is it I, or

is it satan, that is thy enemy? Is it I, or is it thy
carnal self that would undo thee? Is it a holy life,
or a life of sin that thou hast cause to fly from? If
thou be undone, thou procurest this to thyself, by forsaking me, the Lord that would have saved thee."
Jer. 2 : 7. "Doth not thy own wickedness correct
thee, and thy sin reprove thee? Thou mayest see that
it is an evil and bitter thing that thou hast forsaken
me." Jer. 2 : 19. "What iniquity have you found
in me that you have followed after vanity, and forsaken me?" Jer. 2 : 5, 6. He calleth out, as it were,
to the brutes, to hear the controversy he hath against
you. Mic. 2 : 3, 5, "Hear, O ye mountains, the Lord's
controversy, and ye strong foundations of the earth;
for the Lord hath a controversy with his people, and
he will plead with Israel. O my people, what have
I done unto thee, and wherein have I wearied thee?
testify against me, for I brought thee up out of Egypt,
and redeemed thee." "Hear, O heavens, and give
ear, O earth, for the Lord hath spoken. I have nou-
rished and brought up children, and they have rebell-
ed against me. The ox knoweth his owner, and the
ass his master's crib; but Israel doth not know, my
people doth not consider! Ah sinful nation, a people
laden with iniquity, a seed of evil doers!" &c. Isaiah
1 : 2, 4. "Do you thus requite the Lord, O foolish
people, and unwise? Is not he thy Father that bought
thee? Hath he not made thee, and established thee?"
Deut. 32 : 6. When he saw that you forsook him,
even for nothing, and turned away from the Lord of
life to hunt after the chaff and feathers of the world,
he told you of your folly, and called you to a more
profitable employment, Isaiah, 55 : 1, 3. "Wherefore do ye spend your money for that which is not

bread, and your labor for that which satisfieth not? Hearken diligently unto me, and eat ye that which is good, and let your soul delight itself in fatness. Incline your ear, and come unto me; hear, and your soul shall live; and I will make an everlasting covenant with you, even the sure mercies of David. Seek ye the Lord while he may be found: call ye upon him while he is near. Let the wicked forsake his way, and the unrighteous man his thoughts, and let him return unto the Lord, and he will have mercy upon him; and to our God, for he will abundantly pardon;" and so Isa. 1 : 16—18. And when you would not hear, what complaints have you put him to, charging it on you as your wilfulness and stubbornness. Jer. 2 : 13, 13. " Be astonished, O heavens, at this, and be horribly afraid; for my people have committed two evils; they have forsaken me, the fountain of living waters, and hewed them out cisterns, broken cisterns, that can hold no water." Many a time hath Christ proclaimed that free invitation to you, Rev. 22 : 17, " Let him that is athirst come, and whosoever will, let him take the water of life freely." But you put him to complain, after all his offers, " They will not come to me, that they may have life." John, 5 : 40. He hath invited you to feast with him in the kingdom of his grace, and you have had excuses from your grounds, and your cattle, and your worldly business; and when you would not come, you have said you could not, and provoked him to resolve that you should never taste of his supper. Luke, 14 : 16—25. And who is it the fault of now but yourselves? and what can you say is the chief cause of your damnation but your own wills? you would be damned. The whole case is laid open by Christ himself. Prov.

1 : 20—33. " Wisdom crieth without, she uttereth her voice in the streets; she crieth in the chief place of concourse—How long, ye simple ones, will ye love simplicity, and the scorners delight in their scorning, and fools hate knowledge? Turn ye at my reproof. Behold, I will pour out my Spirit upon you, I will make known my words unto you. Because I have called, and ye refused. I have stretched out my hands and no man regarded; but ye have set at naught all my counsels, and would none of my reproofs. I also will laugh at your calamity, I will mock when your fear cometh: when your fear cometh as desolation, and your destruction cometh as a whirlwind; when distress and anguish cometh upon you, then shall they call upon me, but I will not answer; they shall seek me early, but they shall not find me, for that they hated knowledge, and did not choose the fear of the Lord. They would none of my counsels; they despised all my reproofs; therefore shall they eat of the fruit of their own way, and be filled with their own devices. For the turning away of the simple shall slay them, and the prosperity of fools shall destroy them. But whoso hearkeneth to me shall dwell safely, and shall be quiet from the fear of evil." I thought best to recite the whole text at large to you, because it doth so fully show the cause of the destruction of the wicked. It is not because God would not teach them, but because they would not learn. It is not because God would not call them, but because they would not turn at his reproof. Their wilfulness is their undoing.

Use.—From what hath been said, you may further learn these following things:

1. From hence you may see, not only what blas-

phemy and impiety it is to lay the blame of men's
destruction upon God, but also how unfit these wicked
wretches are to bring in such a charge against their
Maker! They cry out upon God, and say he gives
them not grace, and his threatenings are severe, and
God forbid that all should be condemned that be not
converted and sanctified; and they think it hard
measure that a short sin should have an endless suffering; and if they be damned they say they cannot
help it, when, in the meantime, they are busy about
their own destruction, even the destruction of their
own souls, and will not be persuaded to hold their
hands. They think God were cruel if he should condemn them, and yet they are so cruel to themselves
that they will run into the fire of hell, when God hath
told them it is a little before them; and neither en-
treaties, nor threatenings, nor any thing that can be
said, will stop them. We see them almost undone;
their careless, worldly, fleshly lives, tell us that they
are in the power of the devil; we know, if they die
before they are converted, all the world cannot save
them; and knowing the uncertainty of their lives, we
are afraid every day lest they drop into the fire; and
therefore we entreat them to pity their own souls, and
not to undo themselves when mercy is at hand, and
they will not hear us. We entreat them to cast away
their sin, and come to Christ without delay, and to
have some mercy on themselves, but they will have
none; and yet they think that God must be cruel if
he condemn them. O wilful miserable sinners! it is
not God that is cruel to you, it is you that are cruel
to yourselves; you are told you must turn or burn,
and yet you turn not. You are told, that if you will
needs keep your sins, you shall keep the curse of God

with them, and yet you will keep them. You are told
that there is no way to happiness but by holiness, and
yet you will not be holy. What would you have God
say more to you? What would you have him do with
his mercy? He offereth it to you, and you will not
have it. You are in the ditch of sin and misery, and
he would give you his hand to help you out, and you
refuse his help; he would cleanse you of your sins,
and you had rather keep them; you love your lust,
and love your gluttony, and sports, and drunkenness,
and will not let them go; would you have him bring
you to heaven whether you will or not? Or would
you have him bring you and your sins to heaven
together? Why that is an impossibility; you may as
well expect he should turn the sun into darkness.
What! an unsanctified fleshly heart be in heaven?
it cannot be. There entereth nothing that is unclean.
Rev. 21 : 17. " For what communion hath light with
darkness, or Christ with Belial?" 2 Cor. 6 : 14, 15.
" All the day long hath he stretched out his hands to
a disobedient and gainsaying people." Rom. 10 : 21.
What will you do now? Will you cry to God for
mercy? Why, God calleth upon you to have mercy
upon yourselves, and you will not! Ministers see the
poisoned cup in the drunkard's hand, and tell him
there is poison in it, and desire him to have mercy on
his soul, and forbear, and he will not hear us! Drink
it he must and will; he loves it, and, therefore, though
hell comes next, he saith he cannot help it. What
should one say to such men as these? We tell the
ungodly careless worldling, it is not such a life that
will serve the turn, or ever bring you to heaven. If
a lion were at your back you would mend your pace;
when the curse of God is at your back, and satan

and hell are at your back, will you not stir, but ask, What needs of all this ado? Is an immortal soul of no more worth? O have mercy upon yourselves! But they will have no mercy on themselves, nor once regard us. We tell them the end will be bitter. Who can dwell with the everlasting fire? And yet they will have no mercy on themselves. And yet will these shameless transgressors say, that God is more merciful than to condemn them, when it is themselves that cruelly and unmercifully run upon condemnation; and if we should go to them, and entreat them, we cannot stop them; if we should fall on our knees to them we cannot stop them, but to hell they will go, and yet will not believe that they are going thither. If we beg of them for the sake of God that made them, and preserveth them; for the sake of Christ that died for them; for the sake of their own souls to pity themselves, and go no further in the way to hell, but come to Christ while his arms are open, and enter into the state of life while the door stands open, and now take mercy while mercy may be had, they will not be persuaded. If we should die for it, we cannot so much as get them now and then to consider with themselves of the matter, and turn; and yet they can say, " I hope God will be merciful." Did you never consider what he saith, Isa. 27 : 11, " It is a people of no understanding; therefore, he that made them will not have mercy on them, and he that formed them will show them no favor." If another man will not clothe you when you are naked, and feed you when you are hungry, you will say he is unmerciful. If he should cast you into prison, or beat and torment you, you would say he is unmerciful: and yet you will do a thousand

times more against yourselves, even cast away both
soul and body for ever, and never complain of your
own unmercifulness! Yea, and God that waited upon
you all the while with his mercy, must be taken to
be unmerciful, if he punish you after all this. Unless
the holy God of heaven will give these wretches
leave to trample upon his Son's blood, and with the
Jews, as it were, again to spit in his face, and do despite to the spirit of grace, and make a jest of sin, and
a mock at holiness, and set more light by saving
mercy than by the filth of their fleshly pleasures; and
unless, after all this, he will save them by the mercy
which they cast away, and would have none of, God
himself must be called unmerciful by them! But he
will be justified when he judgeth, and he will not
stand or fall at the bar of a sinful worm.

I know there are many particular cavils that are
brought by them against the Lord; but I shall not
here stay to answer them particularly, having done
it already in my *Treatise of Judgment*, to which I
shall refer them. Had the disputing part of the world
been as careful to avoid sin and destruction as they
have been busy in searching after the cause of them,
and forward indirectly to impute them to God, they
might have exercised their wits more profitably, and
have less wronged God, and sped better themselves.
When so ugly a monster as sin is within us, and so
heavy a thing as punishment is on us, and so dreadful
a thing as hell is before us, one would think it should
be an easy question who is in the fault; whether God
or man be the principal or culpable cause? Some
men are such favorable judges of themselves, that
they are more prone to accuse the infinite perfection
and goodness itself, than their own hearts, and imitate

their first parents, that said, " The serpent tempted me ; and the woman that thou gavest me gave unto me, and I did eat ;" secretly implying that God was the cause. So say they, " The understanding that thou gavest me was unable to discern ; the will that thou gavest me was unable to make a better choice ; the objects which thou didst set before me did entice me ; the temptations which thou didst permit to assault me prevailed against me." And some are so loth to think that God can make a self-determining creature, that they dare not deny him that which they take to be his prerogative, to be the determiner of the will in every sin, as the first efficient immediate physical cause ; and many could be content to acquit God from so much causing of evil, if they could but reconcile it with his being the chief cause of good ; as if truths would be no longer truths than we are able to see them in their perfect order and coherence ; because our ravelled wits cannot see them right together, nor assign each truth its proper place, we presume to conclude that some must be cast away. This is the fruit of proud self-conceitedness, when men receive not God's truth as a child his lesson, in holy submission to the omniscience of our Teacher but as censurers that are too wise to learn.

Objection. But we cannot convert ourselves till God convert us ; we can do nothing without his grace ; it is not in him that willeth, nor in him that runneth, but in God that showeth mercy.

Answ. 1. God hath two degrees of mercy to show ; the mercy of conversion first, and the mercy of salvation last ; the latter he will give to none but those that *will* and *run*, and hath promised it to them only. The former is to make them willing that are unwilling; and though your own willingness and endeavors deserve not his grace, yet your wilful refusal deserveth that it should be denied to you. Your disability is your very unwillingness itself, which excuseth not your sin, but maketh it the greater. You could turn if you were but truly willing; and if your wills themselves are so corrupted that nothing but effectual grace will move them, you have the more cause to seek for that grace, and yield to it, and do what you can in the use of means, and not neglect it and set yourself against it. Do what you are able first, and then complain of God for denying you grace, if you have cause.

Object. But you seem to intimate all this while that man hath free will.

Answ. 1. The dispute about free will is beyond your capacity; I shall, therefore, now trouble you with no more but this about it. Your will is naturally a free, that is, a self-determining faculty; but it is viciously inclined, and backward to do good; and therefore we see, by sad experience, that it hath not a virtuous moral freedom; but that it is the wickedness of it which procures the punishment; and I pray you let us not befool ourselves with opinions. Let the case be your own. If you had an enemy that was so malicious as to fall upon you and beat you, or take away the lives of your children, would you excuse him because he said I have not free will; it is my nature, I cannot choose unless God give me grace? If you had a servant that robbed you, would you take such an answer from him? Might not every thief and murderer that is hanged at the assize give such an answer: I have not free will; I cannot change my own heart; what can I do without God's grace? and shall

they therefore be acquitted? If not, why then should
you think to be acquitted for a course of sin against
the Lord?

2. From hence also you may observe these three
things together:—1. What a subtle tempter Satan is.
2. What a deceitful thing sin is. 3. What a foolish
creature corrupted man is. A subtle tempter, indeed,
that can persuade the greatest part of the world to
go into everlasting fire, when they have so many
warnings and dissuasives as they have! A deceitful
thing is sin, indeed, that can bewitch so many thousands to part with everlasting life for a thing so base
and utterly unworthy! A foolish creature is man, indeed, that will be cheated of his salvation for nothing
yea, for a known nothing; and that by an enemy, and
a known enemy. You would think it impossible that
any man in his wits should be persuaded for a little to
cast himself into the fire, or water, or into a coal-pit,
to the destruction of his life; and yet men will be
enticed to cast themselves into hell. If your natural
lives were in your own hands, that you should not die
till you would kill yourselves, how long would most
of you live? And yet, when your everlasting life is so
far in your own hands, under God, that you cannot
be undone till you undo yourselves, how few of you
will forbear your own undoing? Ah, what a silly
thing is man! and what a bewitching and befooling
thing is sin!

3. From hence, also, you may learn, that it is no
great wonder if wicked men be hinderers of others in
the way to heaven, and would have as many unconverted as they can, and would draw them into sin,
and keep them in it. Can you expect that they
should have mercy on others, that have none upon

themselves? and that they should hesitate much at the destruction of others, that hesitate not to destroy themselves? They do no worse by others than they do by themselves.

4. Lastly, You may hence learn that the greatest enemy to man is himself; and the greatest judgment in this life that can befall him, is to be left to himself; that the great work that grace hath to do, is to save us from ourselves; that the greatest accusations and complaints of men should be against themselves, that the greatest work that we have to do ourselves, is to resist ourselves; and the greatest enemy that we should daily pray, and watch, and strive against, is our own carnal hearts and wills; and the greatest part of your work, if you would do good to others, and help them to heaven, is to save them from themselves, even from their blind understandings, and corrupted wills, and perverse affections, and violent passions, and unruly senses. I only name all these for brevity's sake, and leave them to your further consideration.

Well, sirs, now we have found out the great delinquent and murderer of souls, (even men's selves, their own wills,) what remains but that you judge according to the evidence, and confess this great iniquity before the Lord, and be humbled for it, and do so no more? To these three ends distinctly, I shall add a few words more. 1. Further to convince you. 2. To humble you. And, 3. To reform you, if there yet be any hope.

1. We know so much of the exceeding gracious nature of God, who is willing to do good, and delighteth to show mercy, that we have no reason to suspect him of being the culpable cause of our death,

or to call him cruel; he made all good, and he preserveth and maintaineth all; the eyes of all wait
upon him, and he giveth them their meat in due
season; he openeth his hand, and satisfieth the desires of all the living. Psalm 145 : 15, 16. He is not
only righteous in all his ways, and therefore will deal
justly; and holy in all his works, and therefore not
the author of sin, but he is also good to all, and his
tender mercies are over all his works. Psalm 145 :
17, 19.

But as for man, we know his mind is dark, his will
perverse, and his affections carry him so headlong,
that he is fitted by his folly and corruption to such a
work as the destroying of himself. If you saw a
lamb lie killed in the way, would you sooner suspect
the sheep, or the wolf to be the author of it, if they
both stand by? Or if you see a house broken open,
and the people murdered, would you sooner suspect
the prince or judge, that is wise and just, and had no
need, or a known thief or murderer? I say, therefore,
as James, 1 : 13—15, " Let no man say, when he is
tempted, that he is tempted of God, for God cannot
be tempted with evil, neither tempteth he any man,
(to draw him to sin,) but every man is tempted when
he is drawn away of his own lust and enticed. Then
when lust hath conceived, it bringeth forth sin; and
sin, when it is finished, bringeth forth death." You
see here that sin is the offspring of your own concu-
piscence, and not to be charged on God; and that
death is the offspring of your own sin, and the fruit
which it will yield you as soon as it is ripe. You
have a treasure of evil in yourselves, as a spider hath
of poison, from whence you are bringing forth hurt
to yourselves, and spinning such webs as entangle

your own souls. Your nature shows it is you that are the cause.

2. It is evident that you are your own destroyers, in that you are so ready to entertain any temptation almost that is offered to you. Satan is scarcely more ready to move you to any evil, than you are ready to hear, and to do as he would have you. If he would tempt your understanding to error and prejudice, you yield. If he would hinder you from good resolutions, it is soon done. If he would cool any good desires or affections, it is soon done. If he would kindle any lust, or vile affections and desires in you, it is soon done. If he will put you on to evil thoughts, or deeds, you are so free that he needs no rod or spur. If he would keep you from holy thoughts, and words, and ways, a little doth it, you need no curb. You examine not his suggestions, nor resist them with any resolution, nor cast them out as he casts them in, nor quench the sparks which he endeavoreth to kindle ; but you set in with him, and meet him half way, and embrace his motions, and tempt him to tempt you. And it is easy for him to catch such greedy fish that are ranging for a bait, and will take the bare hook.

3. Your destruction is evidently of yourselves, in that you resist all that would help to save you, and would do you good, or hinder you from undoing yourselves. God would help and save you by his word, and you resist it ; it is too strict for you. He would sanctify you by his Spirit, and you resist and quench it. If any man reprove you for your sin, you fly in his face with evil words ; and if he would draw you to a holy life, and tell you of your present danger, you give him little thanks, but either bid him look to himself, he shall not answer for you; or at best you put him off

with heartless thanks, and will not turn when you are persuaded. If ministers would privately instruct and help you, you will not come to them; your unhumbled souls feel but little need of their help; if they would catechise you, you are too old to be catechised, though you are not too old to be ignorant and unholy. What ever they can say to you for your good, you are so self-conceited and wise in your own eyes, even in the depth of ignorance, that you will regard nothing that agreeth not with your present conceits, but contradict your teachers, as if you were wiser than they; you resist all that they can say to you, by your ignorance, and wilfulness, and foolish cavils, and shifting evasions, and unthankful rejections, so that no good that is offered can find any welcome acceptance and entertainment with you.

4. Moreover, it is apparent that you are self-destroyers, in that you " draw the matter of your sin and destruction even from the blessed God himself." You like not the contrivances of his wisdom; you like not his justice, but take it for cruelty; you like not his holiness, but are ready to think he is such a one as yourselves, (Psalm 1 : 21,) and makes as l ght of sin as you do; you like not his truth, but would have his threatenings, even his peremptory threatenings, prove false; and his goodness, which you seem most highly to approve, you partly resist, as it would lead you to repentance; and partly abuse, to the strengthening of your sin, as if you might more freely sin because God is merciful, and because his grace doth so much abound.

5. Yea, you fetch destruction from the blessed Redeemer, and death from the Lord of life himself! and nothing more emboldeneth you in sin, than that

Christ hath died for you; as if now the danger of death were over, and you might boldly venture; as if Christ were become a servant to satan and your sins, and must wait upon you while you are abusing him; and because he is become the Physician of souls, and is able to save to the uttermost all that come to God by him, you think he must suffer you to refuse his help, and throw away his medicines, and must save you whether you will come to God by him or not: so that a great part of your sins are occasioned by your bold presumption upon the death of Christ, not considering that he came to redeem his people from their sins, and to sanctify them a peculiar people to himself, and to conform them in holiness to the image of their heavenly Father, and to their head. Matt. 1 : 21; Tit. 2 : 14; 1 Pet. 1 : 15, 16; Col. 3 : 10, 11; Phil. 3 : 9, 10.

6. You also fetch your own destruction from all the providences and works of God. When you think of his eternal fore-knowledge and decrees, it is to harden you in your sin, or possess your minds with quarrelling thoughts, as if his decrees might spare you the labor of repentance and a holy life, or else were the cause of sin and death. If he afflict you, you repine; if he prosper you, you the more forget him, and are the more backward to the thoughts of the life to come. If the wicked prosper, you forget the end that will set all reckonings straight, and are ready to think it is as good to be wicked as godly; and thus you draw your death from all.

7. And the like you do from all the creatures and mercies of God to you. He giveth them to you as the tokens of his love and furniture for his service, and you turn them against him, to the pleasing of

your flesh. You eat and drink to please your appetite, and not for the glory of God, and to enable you to perform his work. Your clothes you abuse to pride; your riches draw your hearts from heaven; (Phil. 3 : 18;) your honors and applause puff you up; if you have health and strength, it makes you more secure, and forget your end. Yea, other men's mercies are abused by you to your hurt. If you see their honors and dignity, you are provoked to envy them; if you see their riches, you are ready to covet them; if you look upon beauty, you are stirred up to lust; and it is well if godliness itself be not an eye-sore to you.

8. The very gifts that God bestoweth on you, and the ordinances of grace which he hath instituted for his church, you turn to sin. If you have better parts than others, you grow proud and self-conceited; if you have but common gifts, you take them for special grace. You take the bare hearing of your duty for so good a work, as if it would excuse you for not obeying it. Your prayers are turned into sin, because you " regard iniquity in your hearts," (Psalm 66 : 18,) and depart not from iniquity when you call on the name of the Lord. 2 Tim. 2 : 19. Your " prayers are abominable, because you turn away your ear from hearing the law," (Prov. 28 : 9,) and are more ready to offer the sacrifice of fools, thinking you do God some special service, than to hear his word and obey it. Eccles. 5 : 1.

9. Yea, the persons that you converse with, and all their actions, you make the occasions of your sin and destruction. If they live in the fear of God, you hate them. If they live ungodly, you imitate them; if the wicked are many, you think you may the more boldly follow them; if the godly be few, you are the more

emboldened to despise them. If they walk exactly,
you think they are too precise; if one of them fall in
a particular temptation you stumble and turn away
from holiness because that others are imperfectly
holy; as if you were warranted to break your necks
because some others have by their heedlessness strained a sinew, or put out a bone. If a hypocrite discover
himself, you say, " They are all alike," and think
yourselves as honest as the best. A professor can
scarce slip into any miscarriage, but because he cuts
his finger you think you may boldly cut your throats.
If ministers deal plainly with you, you say they rail.
If they speak gently or coldly, you either sleep under
them, or are little more affected than the seats you
sit upon. If any errors creep into the church, some
greedily entertain them, and others reproach the
Christian doctrine for them, which is most against
them. And if we would draw you from any ancient
rooted error, which can but plead two, or three, or six,
or seven hundred years' custom, you are as much
offended with a motion for reformation as if you were
to lose your life by it, and hold fast old errors, while
you cry out against new ones. Scarce a difference
can arise among the ministers of the Gospel, but you
will fetch your own death from it; and you will not
hear, or at least not obey, the unquestionable doctrine
of any of those that agree not with your conceits. One
will not hear a minister because he saith the Lord's
prayer; and another will not hear him because he
doth not use it. One will not hear them that are for
episcopacy; and another will not hear them that are
against it. And thus I might show it you in many
other cases, how you turn all that comes near you to
your own destruction; so clear is it that the ungodly

are self-destroyers, and that their perdition is of themselves.

Methinks now, upon the consideration of what is said, and the review of your own ways, you should bethink you what you have done, and be ashamed and deeply humbled to remember it. If you be not, I pray you consider these following truths:

1. To be your own destroyers is to sin against the deepest principle in your natures, even the principle of self-preservation. Every thing naturally desireth or inclineth to its own felicity, welfare, or perfection, and will you set yourselves to your own destruction? When you are commanded to love your neighbors as yourselves, it is supposed that you naturally love yourselves; but if you love your neighbors no better than yourselves, it seems you would have all the world to be damned.

2. How extremely do you cross your own intentions! I know you intend not your own damnation, even when you are procuring it; you think you are but doing good to yourselves, by gratifying the desires of your flesh. But, alas, it is but as a draught of cold water in a burning fever, or as the scratching of an itching wild-fire, which increaseth the disease and pain. If indeed you would have pleasure, profit, or honor, seek them where they are to be found, and do not hunt after them in the way to hell.

3. What pity is it that you should do that against yourselves which none else on earth or in hell can do! If all the world were combined against you, or all the devils in hell were combined against you, they could not destroy you without yourselves, nor make you sin but by your own consent: and will you do that against yourselves which no one else can do? You have hate-

ful thoughts of the devil, because he is your enemy, and endeavoreth your destruction; and will you be worse than devils to yourselves? Why thus it is with you, if you had hearts to understand it: when you run into sin, and run from godliness, and refuse to turn at the call of God, you do more against your own souls than men or devils could do besides; and if you should set yourselves and bend your wits to do yourselves the greatest mischief, you could not devise to do a greater.

4. You are false to the trust that God hath reposed in you. He hath much intrusted you with your own salvation; and will you betray your trust? He hath set you, with all diligence, to keep your hearts; and is this the keeping of them? Prov. 4 : 23.

5. You do even forbid all others to pity you, when you will have no pity on yourselves. If you cry to God in the day of your calamity for mercy, mercy; what can you expect, but that he should thrust you away, and say, " Nay, thou wouldst not have mercy on thyself; who brought this upon thee but thy own wilfulness?" And if your brethren see you everlastingly in misery, how shall they pity you that were your own destroyers, and would not be dissuaded?

6. It will everlastingly make you your own tormentors in hell, to think that you brought yourselves wilfully to that misery. O what a piercing thought it will be for ever to think with yourselves that this was your own doing! that you were warned of this day, and warned again, but it would not do; that you wilfully sinned, and wilfully turned away from God! that you had time as well as others, but you abused it; you had teachers as well as others, but you refused their instruction; you had holy examples, but

you did not imitate them; you were offered Christ, and grace, and glory, as well as others, but you had more mind of your fleshly pleasures! you had a price in your hands, but you had not a heart to lay it out. Prov. 17 : 16. Can it fail to torment you to think of this your present folly? O that your eyes were open to see what you have done in the wilful wronging of your own souls! and that you better understood these words of God. Prov. 8 : 33, 36, " Hear instruction and be wise, and refuse it not. Blessed is the man that heareth me, watching daily at my gates, waiting at the posts of my doors: for whoso findeth me findeth life, and shall obtain favor of the Lord. But he that sinneth against me, wrongeth his own soul. All they that hate me love death."

And now I am come to the conclusion of this work, my heart is troubled to think how I shall leave you, lest after this the flesh should still deceive you, and the world and the devil should keep you asleep, and I should leave you as I found you, till you awake in hell. Though in care of your poor souls, I am afraid of this, as knowing the obstinacy of a carnal heart; yet I can say with the prophet Jeremiah, (17 : 16,) " I have not desired the woful day, thou Lord knowest." I have not, with James and John, desired that " fire might come from heaven" to consume them that refused Jesus Christ. Luke, 9 : 54. But it is the preventing of the eternal fire that I have been all this while endeavoring: and O that it had been a needless work! That God and conscience might have been as willing to spare me this labor as some of you could have been. Dear friends, I am so loth that you should lie in everlasting fire, and be shut out of hea-

ven, if it be possible to prevent it, that I shall once
more ask you, what do you now resolve? Will you
turn, or die? I look upon you as a physician on his
patient, in a dangerous disease, that saith to him,
" Though you are far gone, take but this medicine,
and forbear but those few things that are hurtful to
you, and I dare warrant your life; but if you will not
do this you are but a dead man." What would you
think of such a man, if the physician, and all the
friends he hath, cannot persuade him to take one medicine to save his life, or to forbear one or two poisonous things that would kill him? This is your case.
As far as you are gone in sin, do but now turn and
come to Christ, and take his remedies, and your souls
shall live. Cast up your deadly sins by repentance,
and return not to the poisonous vomit any more, and
you shall do well. But yet, if it were your bodies
that we had to deal with, we might partly know
what to do for you. Though you would not consent,
yet you might be held or bound while the medicine
were poured down your throats, and hurtful things
might be kept from you. But about your souls it cannot be so; we cannot convert you against your wills.
There is no carrying madmen to heaven in fetters.
You may be condemned against your wills, because
you sinned with your wills; but you cannot be saved
against your wills. The wisdom of God has thought
meet to lay men's salvation or destruction exceedingly much upon the choice of their own will, that
no man shall come to heaven that chose not the way
to heaven; and no man shall come to hell, but shall
be forced to say, " I have the thing I chose, my own
will did bring me hither." Now, if I could but get you
to be willing, to be thoroughly, and resolvedly, and

habitually willing, the work were more than half
done. And alas! must we lose our friends, and must
they lose their God, their happiness, their souls, for
want of this? O God forbid! It is a strange thing
to me that men are so inhuman and stupid in the
greatest matters, who in lesser things are civil and
courteous, and good neighbors. For aught I know, I
have the love of all, or almost all my neighbors, so
far, that if I should send to any man in the town, or
parish, or country, and request a reasonable courtesy
of them, they would grant it me; and yet when I
come to request of them the greatest matter in the
world, for themselves, and not for me, I can have nothing of many of them but a patient hearing. I know
not whether people think a man in the pulpit is in
good earnest or not, and means as he speaks; for I
think I have few neighbors, but, if I were sitting fa-
miliarly with them, and telling them what I have
seen and done, or known in the world, they themselves shall see and know in the world to come, they
would believe me, and regard what I say; but when
I tell them, from the infallible word of God, what they
themselves shall see and know in the world to come,
they show, by their lives, that they do either not believe it or not much regard it. If I met any one of
them on the way, and told them yonder is a coal-pit,
or there is a quicksand, or there are thieves lying in
wait for you, I could persuade them to turn by; but
when I tell them that satan lieth in wait for them,
and that sin is poison to them, and that hell is not a
matter to be jested with, they go on as if they did not
hear me. Truly, neighbors, I am in as good earnest
with you in the pulpit as I am in my familiar discourse; and if ever you will regard me, I beseech

you let it be here. I think there is not a man of you all, but, if my own soul lie at your wills, you would be willing to save it, though I cannot promise that you would leave your sins for it. Tell me, thou drunkard, art thou so cruel to me, that thou wouldst not forbear a few cups of drink, if thou knewest it would save my soul from hell? Hadst thou rather that I did burn there for ever than thou shouldst live soberly as other men do? If so, may I not say, thou art an unmerciful monster, and not a man? If I came hungry or naked to one of your doors, would you not part with more than a cup of drink to relieve me? I am confident you would. If it were to save my life, I know you would, some of you, hazard your own; and yet will you not be entreated to part with your sensual pleasures for your own salvation? Wouldst thou forbear a hundred cups of drink to save my life, if it were in thy power, and wilt thou not do it to save thy own soul? I profess to you, sirs, I am as hearty a beggar with you this day for the saving of your own souls, as I would be for my own supply, if I were forced to come begging to your doors; and therefore if you would hear me then, hear me now. If you would pity me then, be entreated now to pity yourselves. I do again beseech you, as if it were on my bended knees, that you would hearken to your Redeemer, and turn, that you may live. All you that have lived in ignorance, and carelessness, and presumption, to this day; all you that have been drowned in the cares of the world, and have no mind of God, and eternal glory; all you that are enslaved to your fleshly desires of meats and drinks, sports and lusts; and all you that know not the necessity of holiness, and never were acquainted with the sanctifying work of the Holy Ghost upon your souls; that never embraced your blessed Redeemer by a lively faith, and with admiring and thankful apprehensions of his love; and that never felt a higher estimation of God and heaven, and heartier love to them than your fleshly prosperity, and the things below; I earnestly beseech you, not only for my sake, but for the Lord's sake, and for your soul's sake, that you go not one day longer in your former condition, but look about you, and cry to God for converting grace, that you may be made new creatures, and may escape the plagues that are a little before you. And if ever you will do any thing for me, grant me this request, to turn from your evil ways and live. Deny me any thing that ever I shall ask you for myself, if you will but grant me this; and if you deny me this, I care not for any thing else that you would grant me. Nay, as ever you will do any thing at the request of the Lord that made you, and died that you may live, deny him not this; for if you deny him this, he cares for nothing that you shall grant him. As ever you would have him hear your prayers, and grant your requests, and do for you at the hour of death and day of judgment, or in any of your extremities, deny not his request now in the day of your prosperity. O sirs, believe it, death and judgment, and heaven and hell, are other matters when you come near them, than they seem to carnal eyes afar off: then you would hear such a message as I bring you with more awakened regardful hearts.

Well, though I cannot hope so well of all, I will hope that some of you are by this time purposing to turn and live ; and that you are ready to ask me, as the Jews did Peter, (Acts. 2 : 37,) when they were pricked in their hearts, and said, " Men and brethren, what shall we do?" How may we come to be truly converted? We are willing, if we did but know our duty. God forbid that we should choose destruction by refusing conversion, as hitherto we have done.

If these be the thoughts and purposes of your hearts, I say of you as God did of a promising people, (Deut. 5 : 28, 29,) " They have well said all that they have spoken: O that there was such a heart in them, that they would fear me, and keep all my commandments always!" Your purposes are good: O that there were but a heart in you to perform these purposes! And in hope hereof I shall gladly give you direction what to do, and that but briefly, that you may the easier remember it for your practice.

DIRECTION I.—If you would be converted and saved, labor to understand the necessity and true nature of conversion; for what, and from what, and to what, and by what it is that you must turn.

Consider in what a lamentable condition you are till the hour of your conversion, that you may see it is not a state to be rested in. You are under the guilt of all the sins that ever you committed, and under the wrath of God, and the curse of his law; you are bond slaves to the devil, and daily employed in his work against the Lord, yourselves, and others; you are spiritually dead and deformed, as being devoid of the holy life, and nature, and image of the Lord. You are unfit for any holy work, and do nothing that is truly pleasing to God. You are without any promise or assurance of his protection, and live in continual danger of his justice, not knowing what hour you may be snatched away to hell, and most certain to be lost if you die in that condition; and nothing short of conversion can prevent it. Whatever civilities or amendments are short of true conversion, will never procure the saving of your souls. Keep the true sense of this natural misery, and so of the necessity of conversion on your hearts.

And then you must understand what it is to be converted; it is to have a new heart or disposition, and a new conversation.

Quest. 1. For what must we turn?

Answ. For these ends following, which you may attain: 1. You shall immediately be made living members of Christ, and have an interest in him, and be renewed after the image of God, and be adorned with all his graces, and quickened with a new and heavenly life, and saved from the tyranny of Satan, and the dominion of sin, and be justified from the curse of the law, and have the pardon of all the sins of your whole lives, and be accepted of God, and made his sons, and have liberty with boldness to call him Father, and go to him by prayer in all your needs, with a promise of acceptance; you shall have the Holy Ghost to dwell in you, to sanctify and guide you; you shall have part in the brotherhood, communion, and prayers of the saints; you shall be fitted for God's service, and be freed from the dominion of sin, and be useful, and a blessing to the place where you live; and shall have the promise of this life, and that which is to come: you shall want nothing that is truly good for you, and your necessary afflictions you will be enabled to bear; you may have some taste of communion with God in the Spirit, especially in all holy ordinances, where God prepareth a feast for your souls; you shall be heirs of heaven while you live on earth, and may foresee by faith the everlasting glory, and so may live and die in peace; and you shall never be so low but your happiness will be incomparably greater than your misery.

How precious is every one of these blessings, which I do but briefly name, and which in this life you may receive!

And then, 2. At death your souls shall go to Christ, and at the day of judgment both soul and body shall be glorified and justified, and enter into your Master's joy, where your happiness will consist in these particulars:

1. You shall be perfected yourselves; your mortal bodies shall be made immortal, and the corruptible shall put on incorruption; you shall no more be hungry, or thirsty, or weary, or sick, nor shall you need to fear either shame, or sorrow, or death, or hell; your souls shall be perfectly freed from sin, and perfectly fitted for the knowledge, and love, and praises of the Lord.

2. Your employment shall be to behold your glorified Redeemer, with all your holy fellow citizens of heaven, and to see the glory of the most blessed God, and to love him perfectly, and be beloved by him, and to praise him everlastingly.

3. Your glory will contribute to the glory of the New Jerusalem, the city of the living God, which is more than to have a private felicity to yourselves.

4. Your glory will contribute to the glorifying of your Redeemer, who will everlastingly be magnified and pleased in that you are the travail of his soul, and this is more than the glorifying of yourselves.

5. And the eternal Majesty, the living God, will be glorified in your glory, both as he is magnified by

your praises, and as he communicateth of his glory and goodness to you, and as he is pleased in you, and in the accomplishment of his glorious work, in the glory of the New Jerusalem, and of his Son.

All this the poorest beggar of you that is converted shall certainly and endlessly enjoy.

II. You see *for* what you must turn: next you must understand *from* what you must turn; and this is, in a word, from your carnal self, which is the end of all the unconverted:—from the flesh that would be pleased before God, and would still be enticing you;—from the world, that is the bait; and from the devil, that is the angler for souls, and the deceiver. And so from all known and wilful sins.

III. Next you must know to what end you must turn; and that is, to God as your end; to Christ as the way to the Father; to holiness as the way appointed you by Christ; and to the use of all the helps and means of grace afforded you by the Lord.

IV. Lastly; you must know by what you must turn; and that is by Christ, as the only Redeemer and Intercessor; and by the Holy Ghost, as the Sanctifier; and by the word, as his instrument or means; and by faith and repentance, as the means and duties on your part to be performed. All this is of necessity.

DIRECTION II.—If you will be converted and saved, be much in serious secret consideration. Inconsiderateness undoes the world. Withdraw yourselves oft into retired secrecy, and there bethink you of the end why you were made, of the life you have lived, of the time you have lost, the sins you have committed; of the love, and sufferings, and fulness of Christ;

of the danger you are in; of the nearness of death and judgment; of the certainty and excellency of the joys of heaven; and of the certainty and terror of the torments of hell, and the eternity of both; and of the necessity of conversion and a holy life. Absorb your hearts in such considerations as these.

DIRECTION III.—If you will be converted and saved, attend upon the word of God, which is the ordinary means. Read the Scripture, or hear it read, and other holy writings that do apply it; constantly attend on the public preaching of the word. As God will light the world by the sun, and not by himself without it, so will he convert and save men by his ministers, who are the lights of the world. Acts, 26 : 17, 18. Matt. 5 : 14. When he had miraculously humbled Paul, he sent Ananias to him, (Acts, 9 : 10,) and when he had sent an angel to Cornelius, it was but to bid him send for Peter, who must tell him what to believe and do.

DIRECTION IV.—Betake yourselves to God in a course of earnest constant prayer. Confess and lament your former lives, and beg his grace to illuminate and convert you. Beseech him to pardon what is past, and to give you his Spirit, and change your hearts and lives, and lead you in his ways, and save you from temptation. Pursue this work daily, and be not weary of it.

DIRECTION V.—Presently give over your known and wilful sins. Make a stand, and go that way no farther. Be drunk no more, but avoid the very occasion of it. Cast away your lusts and sinful pleasures with detestation. Curse, and swear, and rail no more; and if you have wronged any, restore, as Zaccheus did; if you will commit again your old sins, what blessing can you expect on the means for conversion?

Direction VI.—Presently, if possible, change your company, if it hath hitherto been bad; not by forsaking your necessary relations, but your unnecessary sinful companions; and join yourselves with those that fear the Lord, and inquire of them the way to heaven. Acts, 9 : 19, 26. Psalm 15 : 4.

Direction VII.—Deliver up yourselves to the Lord Jesus, as the physician of your souls, that he may pardon you by his blood, and sanctify you by his Spirit, by his word and ministers, the instruments of the Spirit. He is the way, the truth, and the life, there is no coming to the Father but by him. John, 14 : 6. Nor is there any other name under heaven by which you can be saved. Acts, 4 : 12. Study, therefore, his person and natures, and what he hath done for you, and what he is to you, and what he will be, and how he is fitted to the full supply of all your necessities.

Direction VIII.—If you mean indeed to turn and live, do it speedily, without delay. If you be not willing to turn to-day, you are not willing to do it at all. Remember, you are all this while in your blood, under the guilt of many thousand sins, and under God's wrath, and you stand at the very brink of hell; there is but a step between you and death : and this is not a case for a man that is well in his wits to be quiet in. Up therefore presently, and fly as for your lives, as you would be gone out of your house if it were all on fire over your head. O, if you did but know in what continual danger you live, and what daily unspeakable loss you sustain, and what a safer and sweeter life you might live, you would not stand trifling, but presently turn. Multitudes miscarry that wilfully delay when they are convinced that it must be done. Your lives are short and uncertain; and what a case are you in if you die before you thoroughly turn! Ye have staid too long already, and wronged God too long. Sin getteth strength while you delay. Your conversion will grow more hard and doubtful. You have much to do, and therefore put not all off to the last, lest God forsake you, and give you up to yourselves, and then you are undone for ever.

DIRECTION IX.—If you will turn and live, do it unreservedly, absolutely, and universally. Think not to capitulate with Christ, and divide your heart between him and the world; and to part with some sins and keep the rest; and to let that go which your flesh can spare. This is but self-deluding; you must in heart and resolution forsake all that you have, or else you cannot be his disciples. Luke, 14 : 26, 33. If you will not take God and heaven for your portion, and lay all below at the feet of Christ, but you must needs also have your good things here, and have an earthly portion, and God and glory are not enough for you; it is vain to dream of salvation on these terms; for it will not be. If you seem never so religious, if yet it be but a carnal righteousness, and if the flesh's prosperity, or pleasure, or safety, be still excepted in your devotedness to God, this is as certain a way to death as open profaneness, though it be more plausible.

DIRECTION X.—If you will turn and live, do it resolvedly, and stand not still deliberating, as if it were
a doubtful case. Stand not wavering, as if you were
uncertain whether God or the flesh be the better master, or whether sin or holiness be the better way, or
whether heaven or hell be the better end. But away
with your former lusts, and presently, habitually,
fixedly resolve. Be not one day of one mind, and the
next day of another; but be at a point with all the
world, and resolvedly give up yourselves and all you
have to God. Now, while you are reading, or hearing this, resolve; before you sleep another night, resolve; before you stir from the place, resolve; before
satan have time to take you off, resolve. You never
turn indeed till you do resolve, and that with a firm
unchangeable resolution.

————

And now I have done my part in this work, that
you may turn to the call of God, and live. What will
become of it I cannot tell. I have cast the seed at
God's command; but it is not in my power to give
the increase. I can go no further with my message;
I cannot bring it to your heart, nor make it work; I
cannot do your parts for you to entertain it and consider it; nor can I do God's part, by opening your
heart to entertain it; nor can I show heaven or hell
to your sight, nor give you new and tender hearts. If
I knew what more to do for your conversion, I hope I
should do it.

But O thou that art the gracious Father of spirits,
thou hast sworn thou delightest not in the death of
the wicked, but rather that they turn and live; deny

not thy blessing to these persuasions and directions, and suffer not thine enemies to triumph in thy sight, and the great deceiver of souls to prevail against thy Son, thy Spirit, and thy Word! O pity poor unconverted sinners, that have no hearts to pity or help themselves! Command the blind to see, and the deaf to hear, and the dead to live, and let not sin and death be able to resist thee. Awaken the secure, resolve the unresolved, confirm the wavering; and let the eyes of sinners, that read these lines, be next employed in weeping over their sins, and bring them to themselves, and to thy Son, before their sins have brought them to perdition. If thou say but the word, these poor endeavors shall prosper to the winning of many a soul to their everlasting joy and thine everlasting glory.—*Amen.*